This Book Belongs to

SCAN TO VISIT MY AUTHOR PAGE

Join our Ministry group on facebook

https://www.facebook.com/groups/myholytrinity.co

Check out our merch at

https://fashionsbyfelicia.myecomshop.com

This book is dedicated to my Dad who taught me to be an independent and

determined person, without whom I would never be able to achieve

my dreams

ABOUT THE AUTHOR

Hello, God's children my name is Felicia Patterson, I hold a degree in psychology, aromatherapy as well as am an Ordained Minister. Journaling has helped me through some very tough times in my life along with my faith and I thought why not combine the two. I could go on about my accomplishments but instead, I would like to share with you a personal story of what the power of faith and prayer can do.

ABOUT THE AUTHOR

I was born with a rare spinal condition. My parents reached out to all the greats, but all said there was no treatment and just keep me comfortable until my time came. After months of searching and praying, a young and brilliant neurosurgeon came up with a plan that would hopefully work. Prior to what was to be a series of surgeries, I wanted to see the Happy Hunters that were a few hours away from us. Things were tight but my parents made it happen but only had fifty dollars to travel on. We got to the motel got cleaned up and walked across the street where they were giving the sermon. At this time, I had lost all function of my lower extremities and I had to be carried into the church. Prior to the sermon, they were passing the plate. We only had enough to get back home, so we don't have anything to spare. As they were passing the plate my mom put the fifty dollars in. The lady minister whom I will never forget asked my dad to sit me beside her. While her husband was giving the sermon, she was rubbing my back. My parents had communicated with them through email, but she had no knowledge of who we were or my condition. After a while, she asked my mom and another woman to take my hands and walk me around the church. I had not walked in months yet practically ran around the church. After it was over, we were headed for the lobby when the same woman that walked with me around the church came up to my mom and said, "God told me to give you this" and gave her two twenties and a ten. Our Life is a testament that through all the challenges, loss, and despair that we must hold to our faith and trust that we are all here for a purpose.

Table of Contents

Anger

Ephesians 4:26-27.....14
Proverbs 14:29.....18

Blessings

Exodus 23:25 22
Psalm 20:4 26

Compassion

Lamentations 3:22-23.....30
John 16:24.....34

Confession

James 5:16.....38
Proverbs 28:13.....42

Courage

Joshua 1:9.....46
John14:27.....50

Creation

Genesis 2:3.....54
Jeremiah 32:17.....58

Death

Roman 14:8.....62
Luke 23:46.........66

Encouragement

Deuteronomy 31:8.....70
Luke 23:46.....74

Faith

Romans 15:13.....79
John 11:40.....82

Forgivness

Proverbs 17:19.....86
Colossians 3:13.....90

Fear

Isaiah 41:10.....98
Psalm 27:1.....102

Friendship

1 John 4:7.....101
1 John 4:21........106

Generosity

2 Corinthians 9:7...... 110
James 1:5...... 113

Hope

Jeremiah 29:11.....121
Psalm 121:8-8 125

Table of Contents

Idols

Deuteronomy 4:39......**129**
John 17:15......**133**

Joy

1 Thessalonians 5:16-18......**137**
Psalm 16:11......**141**

Laws

Romans 6:15-......**145**
1 Corinthians 10:23......**149**

Mercy

Hebrews 4:16......**153**
Ephesians 2:4-5......**157**

Neighbors

Mark 12:31......**161**
1 Peter 3:8 ...... **165**

Obedience

Proverbs 6:20......**169**
Proverbs 10:17 ......**173**

Patience

Proverbs 14:29......**177**
Romans 15:5......**181**

Reliability

Deuteronomy 7:9......**185**
Hebrews 10:23......**189**

Self Control

Proverbs 25:28......**193**
2 Timothy 1:7......**197**

Trust

Proverbs 3:5-6......**201**
Proverbs 16:3......**205**

Understanding

Jeremiah 33:3......**209**
Proverbs 4:7......**213**

Bonus Week

Weakness

2 Corinthians 12:10......**217**
Matthew 11:28......**221**

About your journal

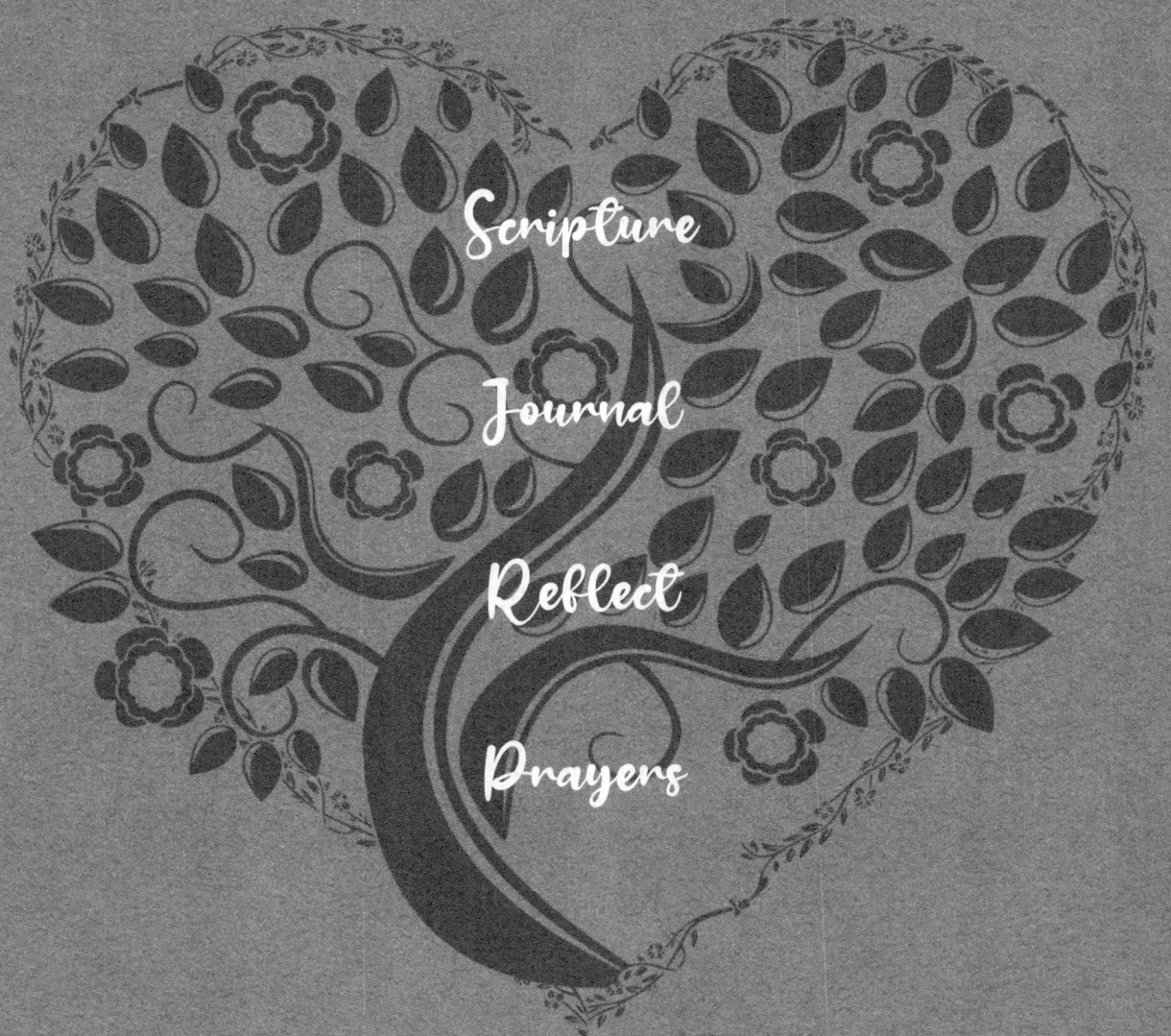

Scripture

Journal

Reflect

Prayers

THE NEXT FEW PAGES WILL EXPLAIN HOW TO

USE YOUR JOURNAL

PSALMS 102

Hear my prayer, Lord;
let my cry for help come to you.
Do not hide your face from me
when I am in distress.
Turn your ear to me;
when I call, answer me quickly.
For my days vanish like smoke;
my bones burn like glowing embers.
My heart is blighted and withered like grass;
I forget to eat my food.
In my distress I groan aloud
and am reduced to skin and bones.
I am like a desert owl,
like an owl among the ruins.
I lie awake; I have become
like a bird alone on a roof.
All day long my enemies taunt me;
those who rail against me use my name as a curse.
For I eat ashes as my food
and mingle my drink with tears
because of your great wrath,
for you have taken me up and thrown me aside.
My days are like the evening shadow;
I wither away like grass.
But you, Lord, sit enthroned forever;
your renown endures through all generations.
You will arise and have compassion on Zion,
for it is time to show favor to her;
the appointed time has come.
For her stones are dear to your servants;
her very dust moves them to pity.
The nations will fear the name of the Lord,
all the kings of the earth will revere your glory.
For the Lordwill rebuild Zion
and appear in his glory.
He will respond to the prayer of the destitute;
he will not despise their plea.
Let this be written for a future generation,
that a people not yet created may praise the Lord:

Scripture

Each week 52 total plus a bonus features a new Scripture to reflect your thoughts on throughout the week giving you time to memorize the verse and understand its true meaning

Journal

What week is it? Record the date and watch how your journey with Gods grows through the year.

What areas of your life you want to grow? Ask god to teach me.

Let God know how grateful you are. What are you thankful for this week?

What are some areas you need God's guidance? Ask for him to guide you.

Reflect

Each week also contains a "Reflect" page with questions and thoughts inspired by the weekly Scripture, as well as room to write down your thoughts. You can use this as a weekly reflection or just fill in the blanks in a single day! Remember that this journal can be customized to fit your spiritual journey.

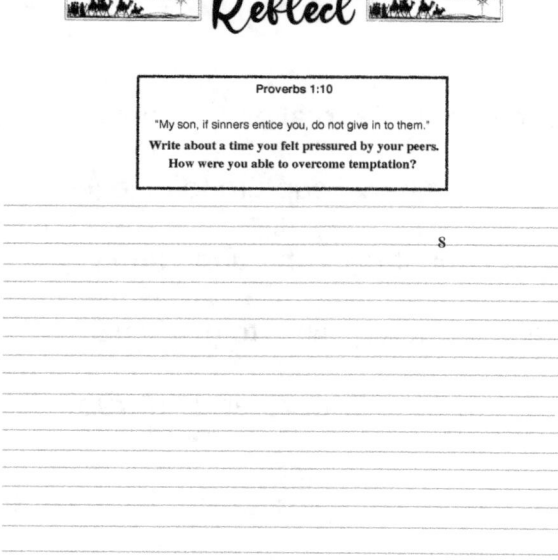

Memories, Prayers and Guidance

It's our job to guide the next generation. What do you want the future generation to know?

Record your weekly prayers.

Life is a beautiful and challenging journey. Take time to write about the

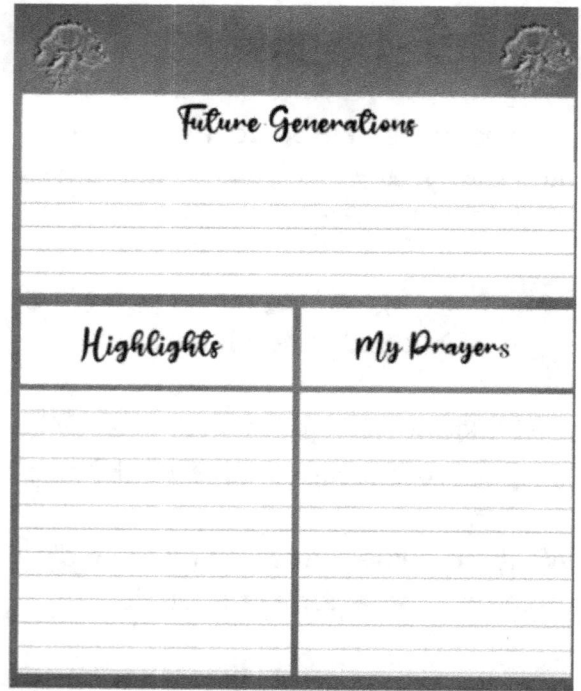

Prayers

The back of the book includes a place to
record your prayers.

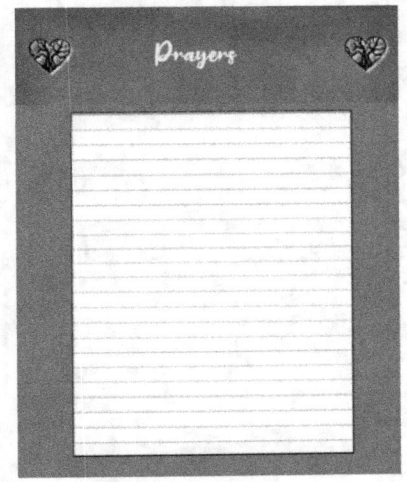

Now that you know how to use your journal, trust
that the Lord will guide you with the year ahead.

EPHESIANS 4:26-27

"BE YE ANGRY, AND SIN NOT: LET

NOT THE SUN GO DOWN UPON

YOUR WRATH: NEITHER GIVE PLACE

TO THE DEVIL".

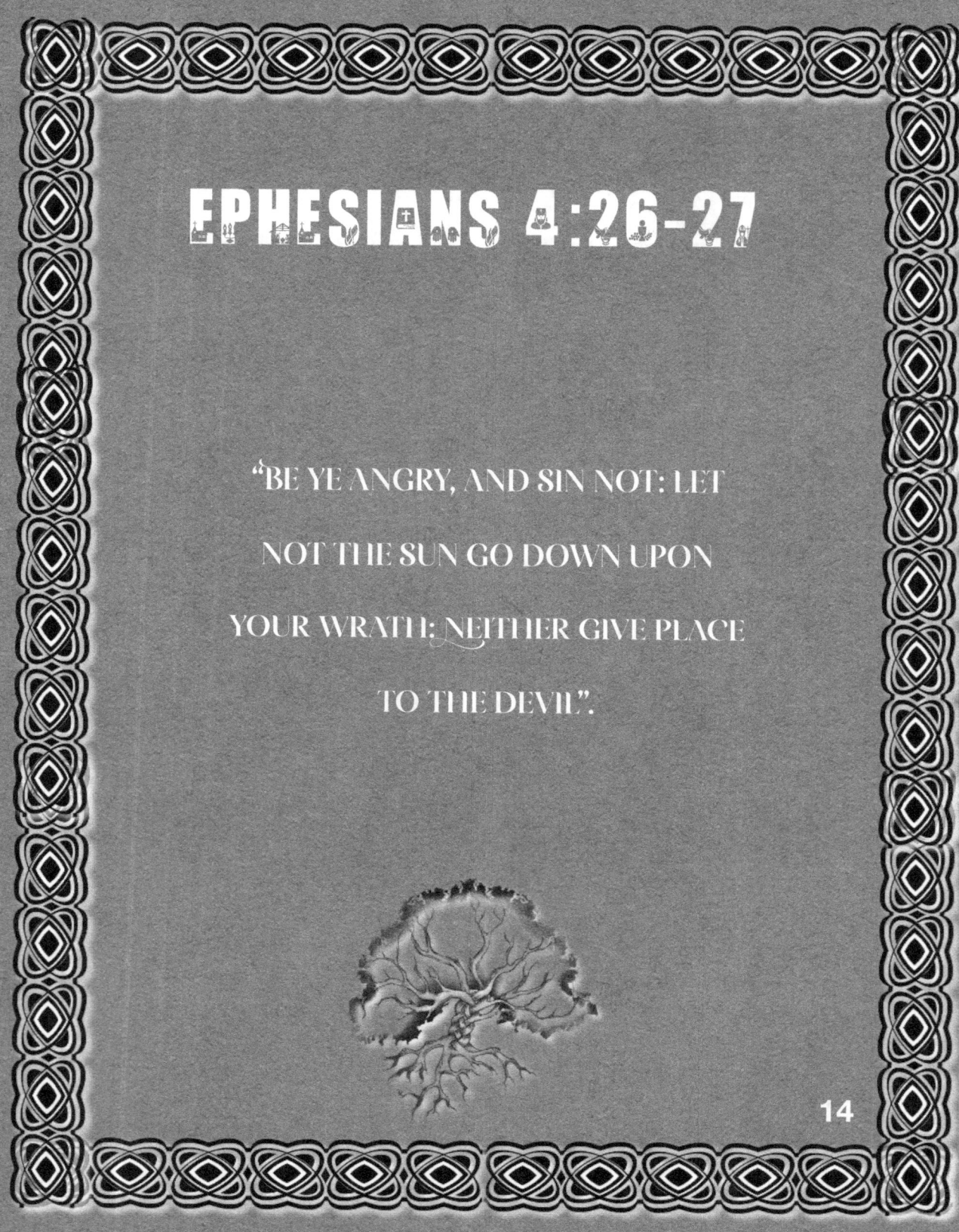

Thank You Lord

Week of: _____

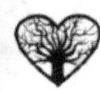 # Teach Me

_____
_____
_____
_____
_____
_____
_____
_____

 # Guide Me

_____
_____
_____
_____
_____
_____
_____
_____

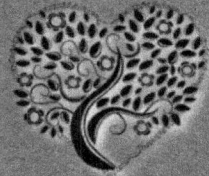

 # Reflect

" What does it mean to you to be a person of faith? How
important is this to you?

_____
_____
_____
_____
_____
_____
_____
_____
_____
_____
_____
_____
_____
_____
_____
_____
_____
_____

Future Generations

Highlights

My Prayers

PROVERBS 14:29

"HE THAT IS SLOW TO WRATH IS OF

GREAT UNDERSTANDING:

BUT HE THAT IS HASTY OF SPIRIT

EXALTETH FOLLY.

"

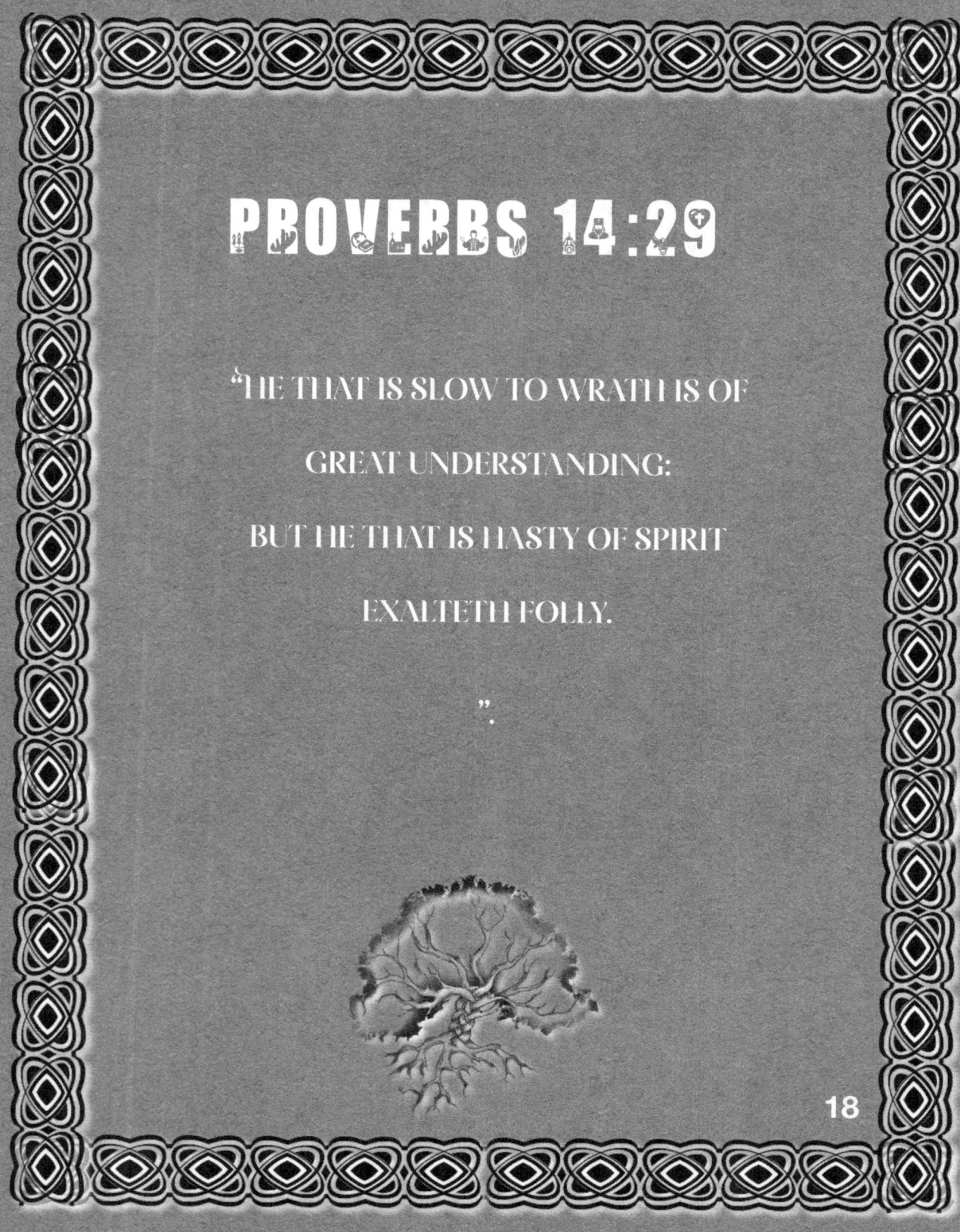

Thank You Lord

Week of: _____

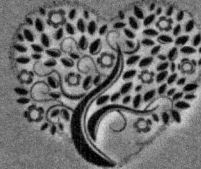

Teach Me

Guide Me

 # Reflect

What's your favorite Bible story about faith? Why?

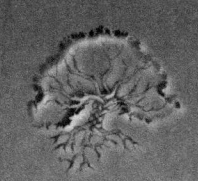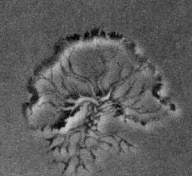

Future Generations

Highlights

My Prayers

EXODUS 23:25

"YE SHALL SERVE THE LORD YOUR GOD, AND HE SHALL BLESS THY BREAD, AND THY WATER; AND I WILL TAKE SICKNESS AWAY FROM THE MIDST OF THEE".

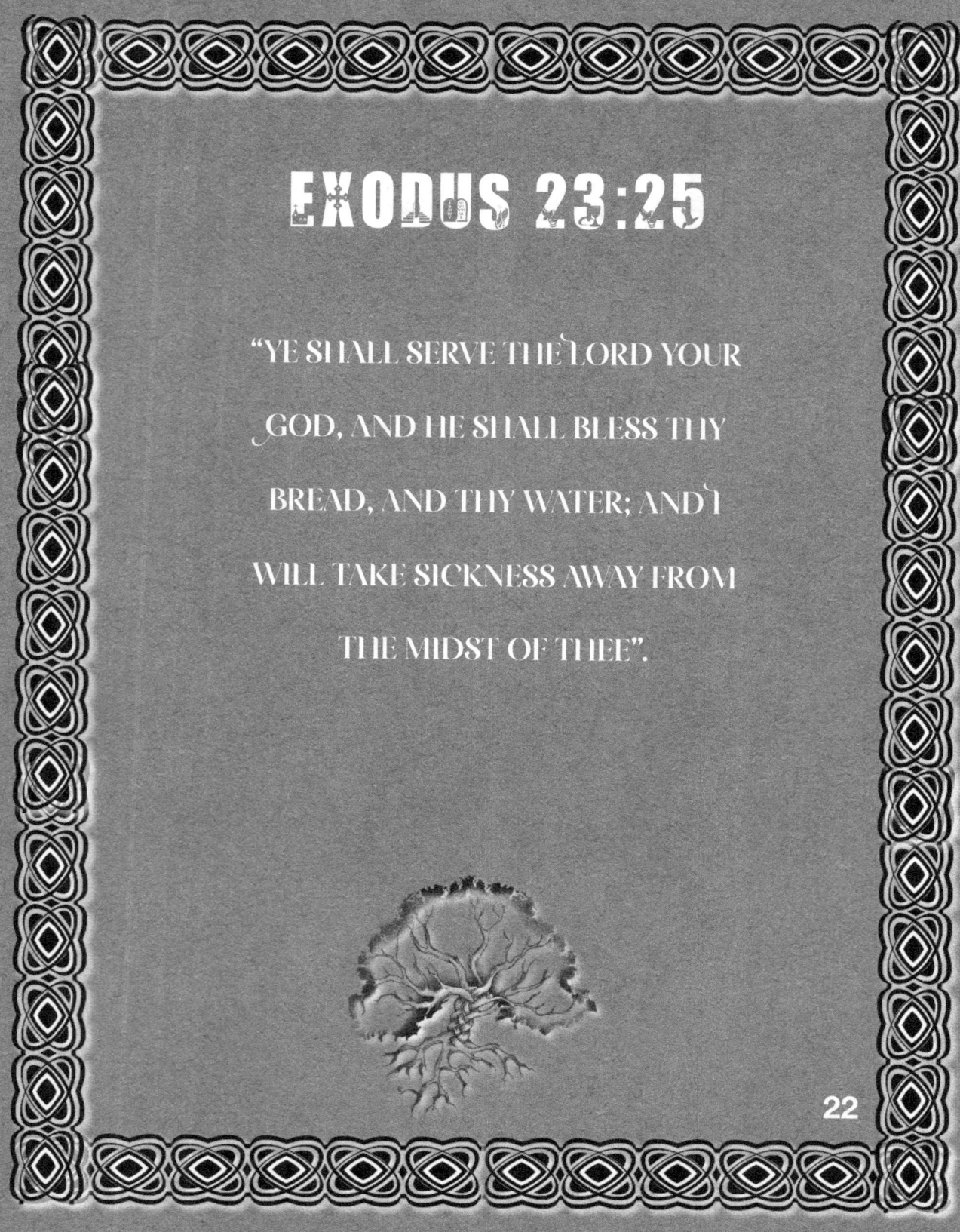

Thank You Lord

Week of: _____

 # Teach Me

_____
_____
_____
_____
_____
_____
_____
_____
_____
_____

Guide Me

_____
_____
_____
_____
_____
_____
_____
_____
_____

 # Reflect

Colossians 4:6

"Let your conversation be always full of grace, seasoned with salt, so that you may know how to answer everyone."

How do you respond to someone who asks you about your faith? How do you share the Word of God?

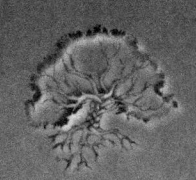 

Future Generations

Highlights

My Prayers

PSALM 20:4

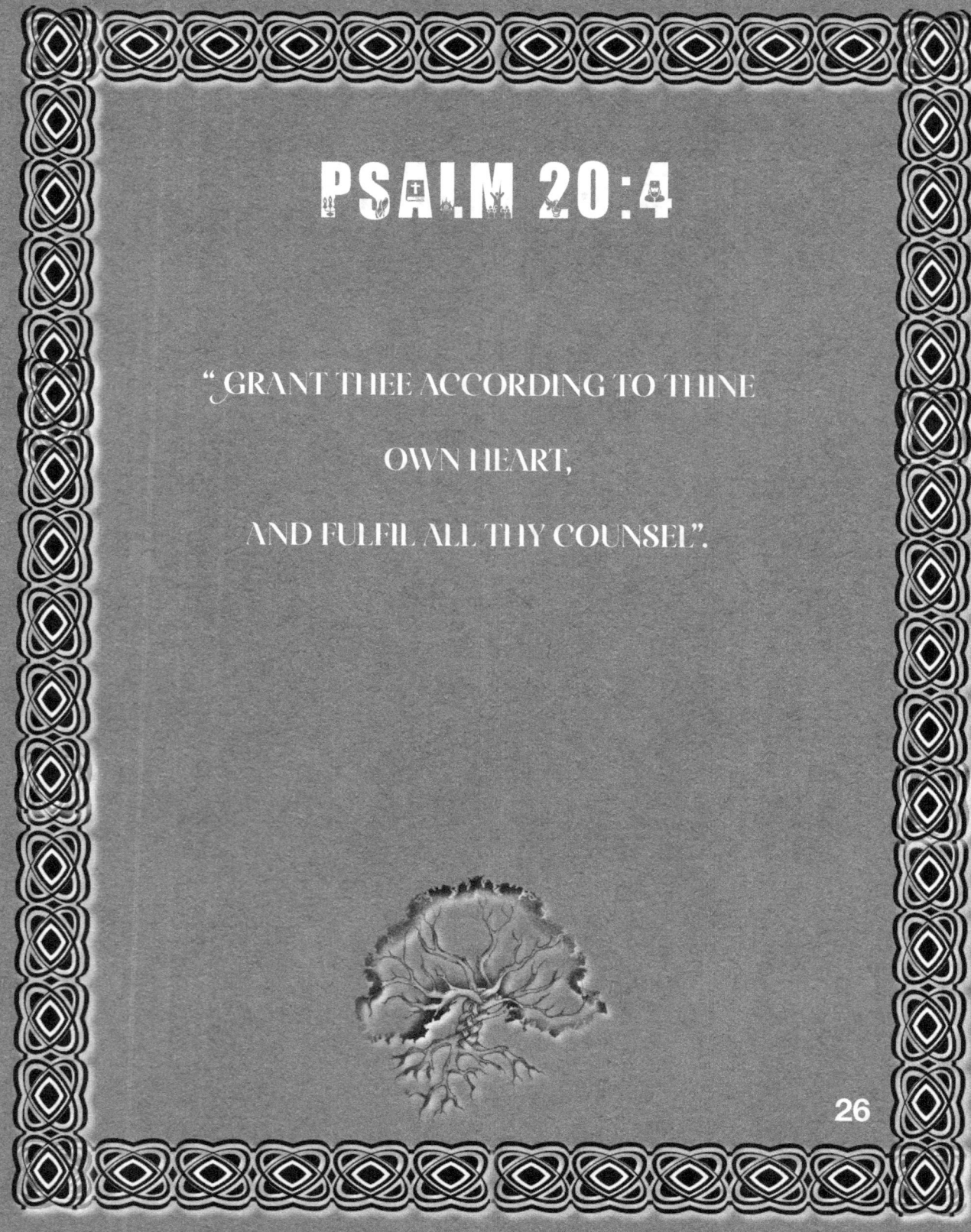

" GRANT THEE ACCORDING TO THINE

OWN HEART,

AND FULFIL ALL THY COUNSEL".

Thank You Lord

Week of: _____

 Teach Me

_____
_____
_____
_____
_____
_____
_____
_____
_____
_____
_____
_____

 Guide Me

_____
_____
_____
_____
_____
_____
_____
_____
_____
_____
_____
_____

 # Reflect

When you think of fear and doubt, which Bible character pops into your mind? How did they overcome (if at all)? What can you learn from them?

_____
_____
_____
_____
_____
_____
_____
_____
_____
_____
_____
_____
_____
_____
_____
_____
_____
_____
_____

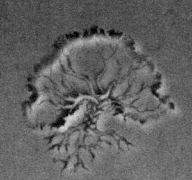

Future Generations

Highlights

My Prayers

LAMENTATIONS 3:22-23

"IT IS OF THE LORD'S MERCIES THAT WE

ARE NOT CONSUMED,

BECAUSE HIS COMPASSIONS FAIL NOT.

THEY ARE NEW EVERY MORNING:

GREAT IS THY FAITHFULNESS"

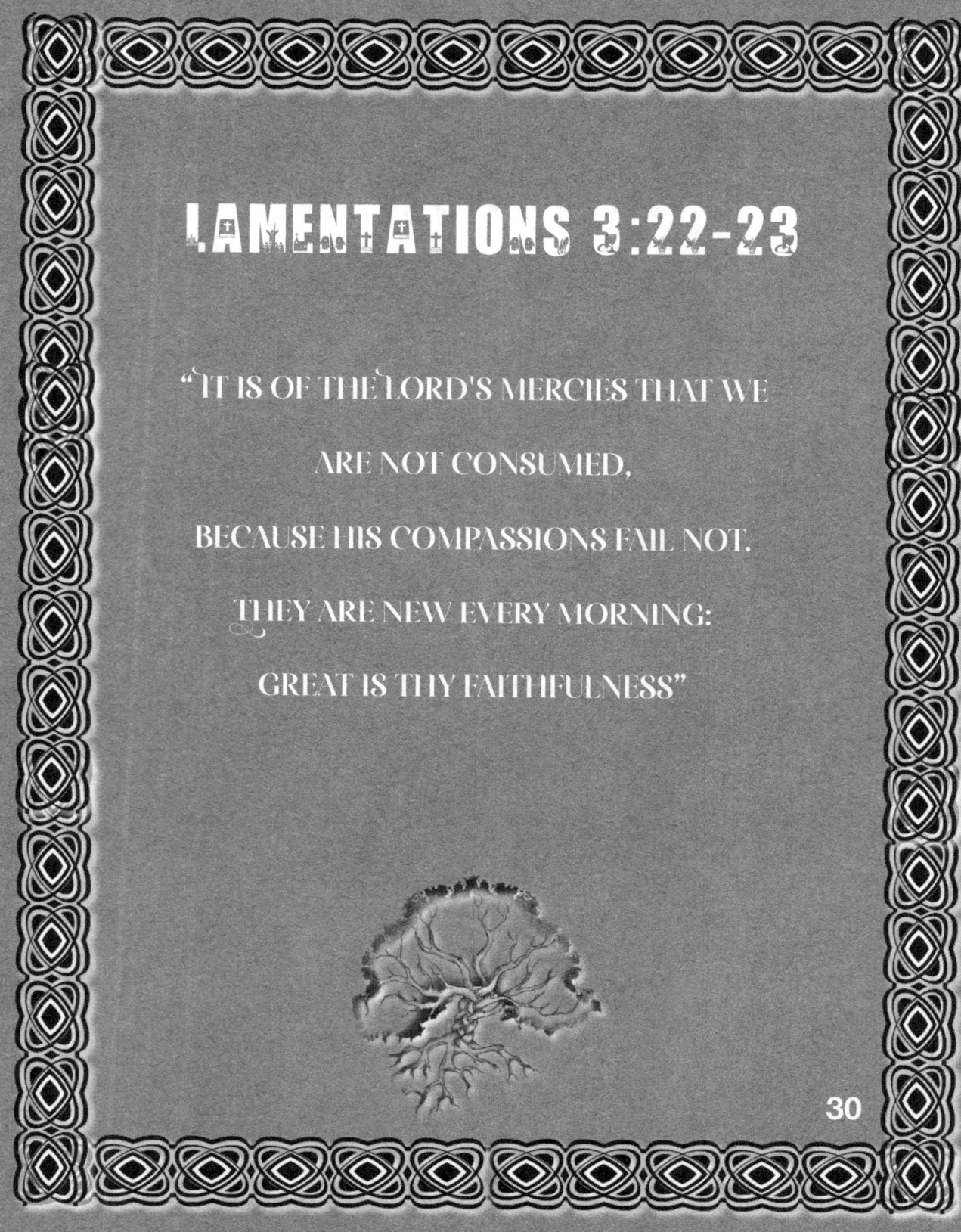

Thank You Lord

Week of: _____

 # Teach Me

_____
_____
_____
_____
_____
_____
_____
_____
_____
_____
_____

Guide Me

_____
_____
_____
_____
_____
_____
_____
_____
_____
_____

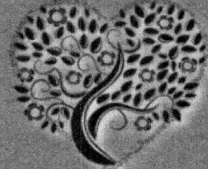

 # Reflect

Job 8:7
"Your beginnings will seem humble, so prosperous will your future be"

Think about something that was challenging for you at first but

through hard work and faith, you have improved your skills?

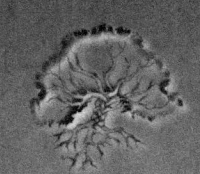

Future Generations

Highlights

My Prayers

EPHESIANS 4:32

"BE YE KIND ONE TO ANOTHER,

TENDERHEARTED, FORGIVING ONE

ANOTHER, EVEN AS GOD FOR CHRIST'S

SAKE HATH FORGIVEN YOU".

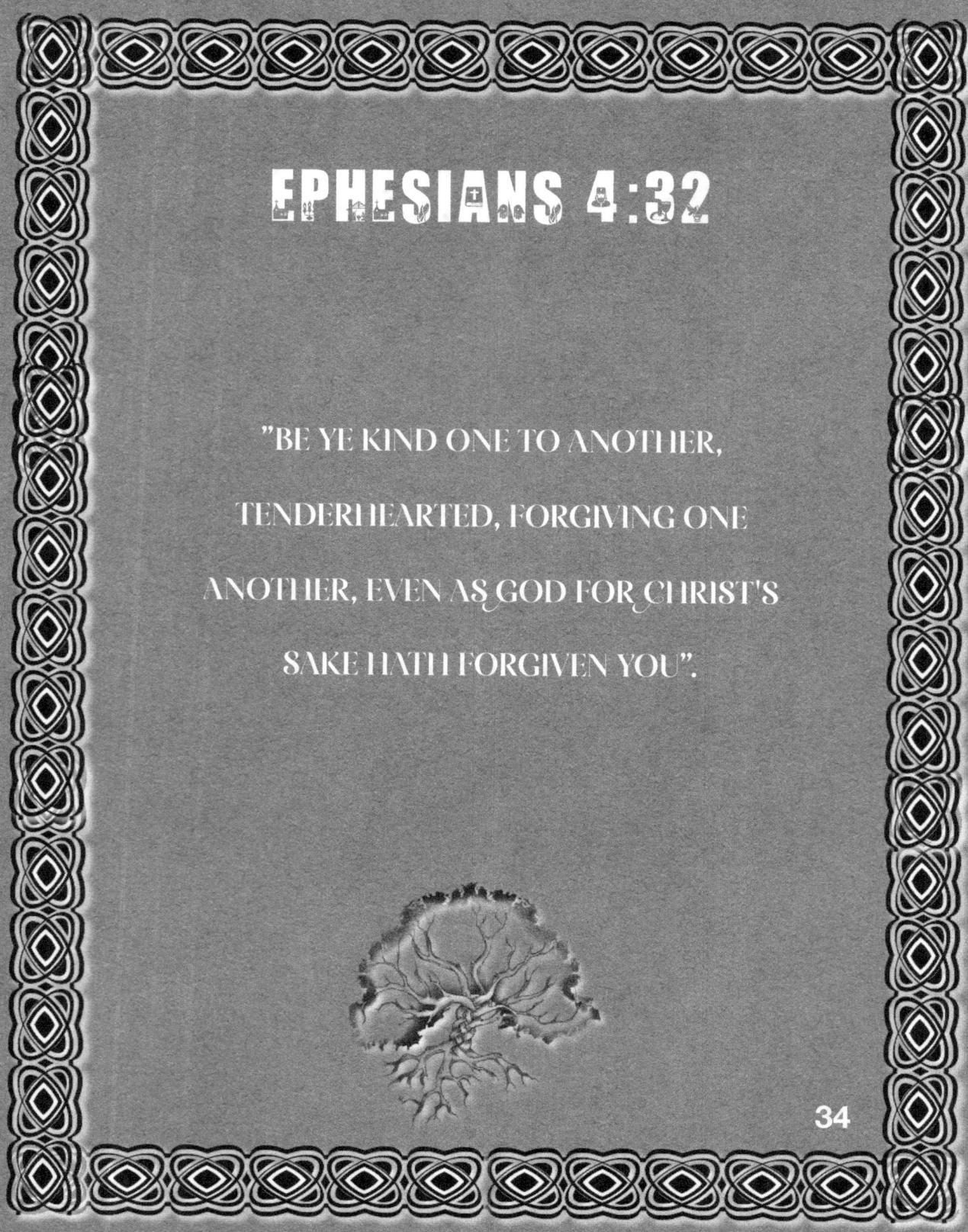

Thank You Lord

Week of: _____

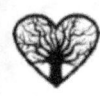 # Teach Me

_____
_____
_____
_____
_____
_____
_____
_____
_____
_____
_____
_____

 # Guide Me

_____
_____
_____
_____
_____
_____
_____
_____
_____
_____

 # Reflect

In what ways have you heard people say

God talks to them? Describe those way

_____
_____
_____
_____
_____
_____
_____
_____
_____
_____
_____
_____
_____
_____
_____
_____
_____
_____
_____
_____
_____
_____

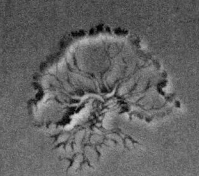 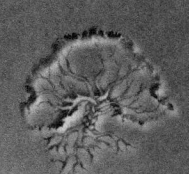

Future Generations

Highlights

My Prayers

JAMES 5:16

"CONFESS YOUR FAULTS ONE TO ANOTHER, AND PRAY ONE FOR ANOTHER, THAT YE MAY BE HEALED. THE EFFECTUAL FERVENT PRAYER OF A RIGHTEOUS MAN AVAILETH MUCH"

Thank You Lord

Week of: _____

 # Teach Me

_____
_____
_____
_____
_____
_____
_____
_____
_____
_____
_____
_____

 # Guide Me

_____
_____
_____
_____
_____
_____
_____
_____
_____

 # Reflect

> ### Matthew 6:25-26
> "Therefore I tell you, do not worry about your life, what you will eat or drink; or about your body, what you will wear. Is not life more than food, and the body more than clothes? Look at the birds of the air; they do not sow or reap or store away in barns, and yet your heavenly Father feeds them. Are you not much more valuable than they?"
>
> **Think about some things you are worried about. Write them down, and then let them go to God.**

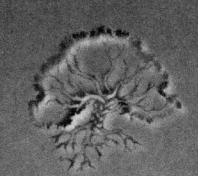
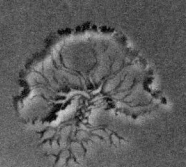

Future Generations

Highlights

My Prayers

PROVERBS 28:13

"HE THAT COVERETH HIS SINS SHALL NOT

PROSPER:

BUT WHOSO CONFESSETH AND

FORSAKETH THEM SHALL HAVE MERCY.

".

Thank You Lord

Week of: _____

 # Teach Me

_____
_____
_____
_____
_____
_____
_____
_____
_____
_____

 # Guide Me

_____
_____
_____
_____
_____
_____
_____
_____
_____

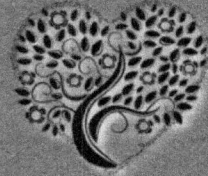

 # Reflect

1 Timothy 4:12

"Don't let anyone look down on you because you are young, but set an example

for the believers in speech, in conduct, in love, in faith and in purity"

How can you overcome stereotypes people hold about you?

_____

_____

_____

_____

_____

_____

_____

_____

_____

_____

_____

_____

_____

_____

_____

_____

_____

_____

_____

_____

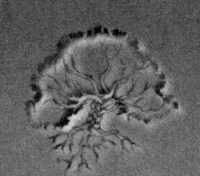

Future Generations

Highlights

My Prayers

JOSHUA 1:9

"HAVE NOT I COMMANDED THEE? BE

STRONG AND OF A GOOD COURAGE; BE NOT

AFRAID, NEITHER BE THOU DISMAYED: FOR

THE LORD THY GOD IS WITH THEE

WHITHERSOEVER THOU GOEST"

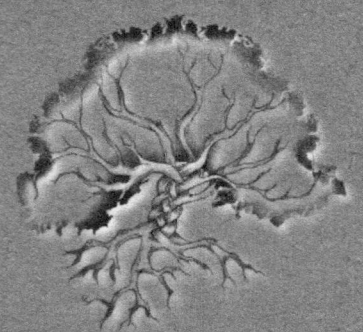

46

Thank You Lord

Week of: _____

 # Teach Me

_____
_____
_____
_____
_____
_____
_____
_____
_____
_____

 # Guide Me

_____
_____
_____
_____
_____
_____
_____
_____

 # Reflect

Apart from the Bible, what book(s) has impacted your

faith greatly? What lessons still resonate with you?

_____
_____
_____
_____
_____
_____
_____
_____
_____
_____
_____
_____
_____
_____
_____
_____
_____
_____
_____
_____
_____
_____

Future Generations

Highlights

My Prayers

JOHN 14:27

"PEACE I LEAVE WITH YOU, MY PEACE I

GIVE UNTO YOU: NOT AS THE WORLD

GIVETH, GIVE I UNTO YOU. LET NOT YOUR

HEART BE TROUBLED, NEITHER LET IT BE

AFRAID".

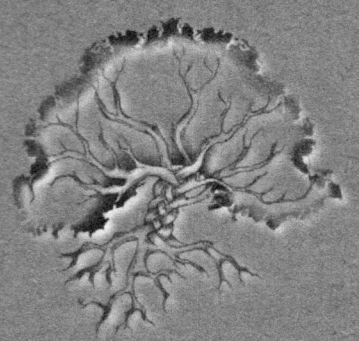

Thank You Lord

Week of: _____

 # Teach Me

_____
_____
_____
_____
_____
_____
_____
_____
_____
_____
_____

 # Guide Me

_____
_____
_____
_____
_____
_____
_____
_____
_____

 # Reflect

Scripture says faith is a gift. How are you sure that you have

accepted that gift?

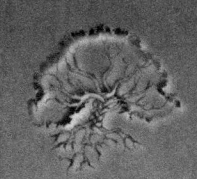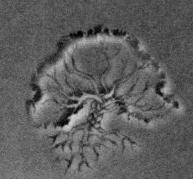

Future Generations

Highlights

My Prayers

GENESIS 2:3

"GOD BLESSED THE SEVENTH DAY, AND SANCTIFIED IT: BECAUSE THAT IN IT HE HAD RESTED FROM ALL HIS WORK WHICH GOD CREATED AND MADE".

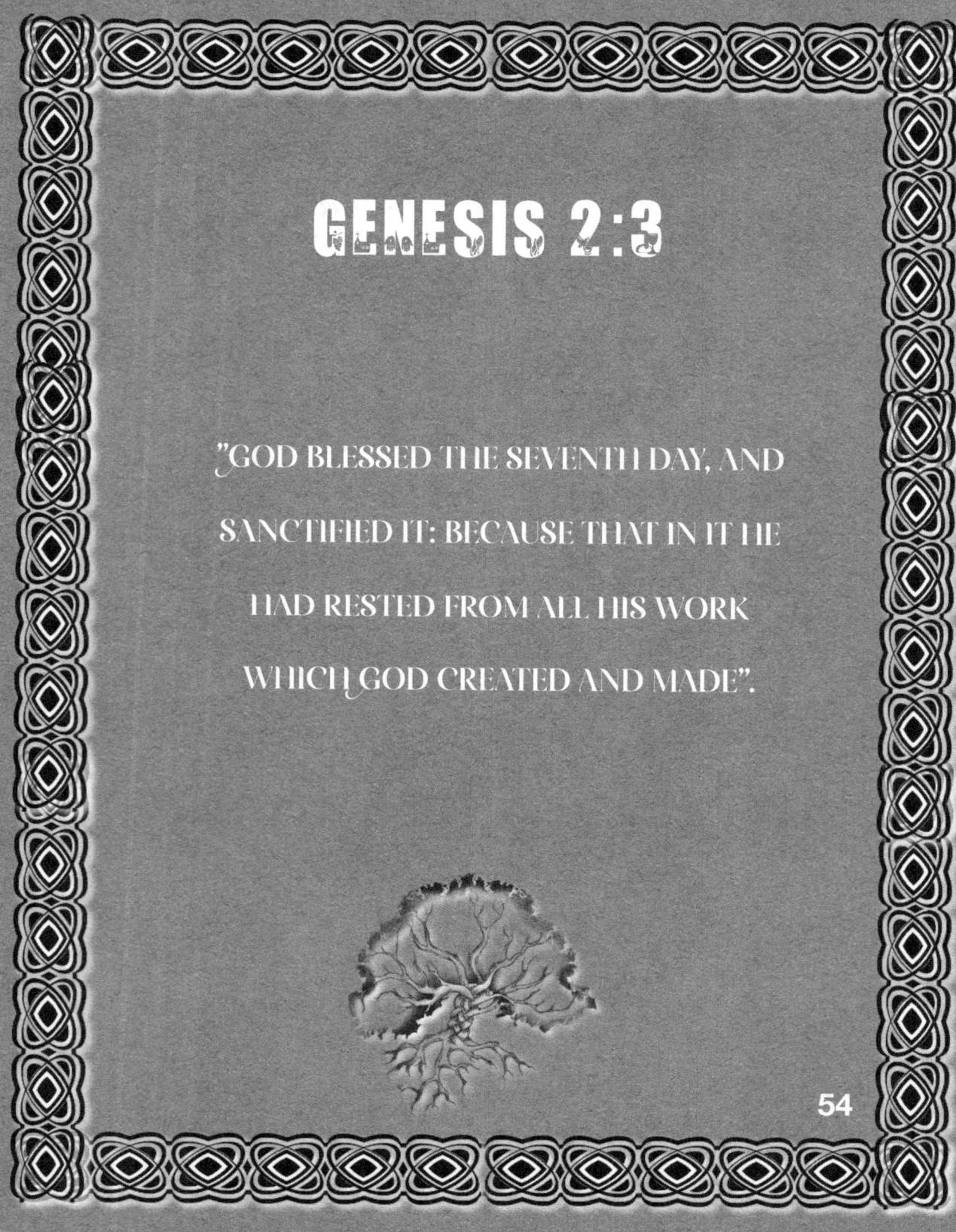

Thank You Lord

Week of: _____

 # Teach Me

_____
_____
_____
_____
_____
_____
_____
_____
_____

 # Guide Me

_____
_____
_____
_____
_____
_____
_____
_____

 # Reflect

Have you ever heard God's voice and was disobedient? What were the consequences? How was your faith strengthened or weakened as a result?

_____

_____

_____

_____

_____

_____

_____

_____

_____

_____

_____

_____

_____

_____

_____

_____

_____

_____

_____

_____

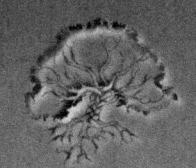
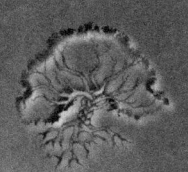

Future Generations

Highlights

My Prayers

JEREMIAH 32:17

"AH LORD GOD! BEHOLD, THOU HAST MADE THE HEAVEN AND THE EARTH BY THY GREAT POWER AND STRETCHED OUT ARM, AND THERE IS NOTHING TOO HARD FOR THEE".

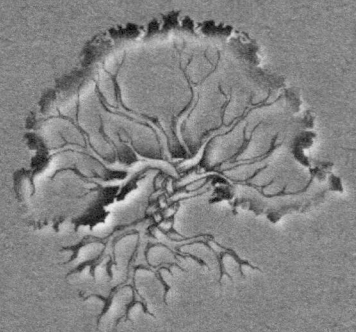

Thank You Lord

Week of: _____

 # Teach Me

_____
_____
_____
_____
_____
_____
_____
_____
_____
_____

 # Guide Me

_____
_____
_____
_____
_____
_____
_____
_____
_____

 # Reflect

> If the Bible were to be rewritten with you as a character
>
> in it, what would you want to be remembered for?

_____

_____

_____

_____

_____

_____

_____

_____

_____

_____

_____

_____

_____

_____

_____

_____

_____

_____

_____

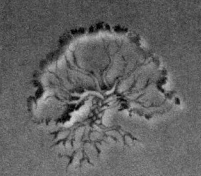 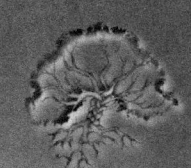

Future Generations

Highlights

My Prayers

ROMANS 14:8

"ENEROSITY FOR WHETHER WE LIVE, WE LIVE UNTO THE LORD; AND WHETHER WE DIE, WE DIE UNTO THE LORD: WHETHER WE LIVE THEREFORE, OR DIE, WE ARE THE LORD'S".

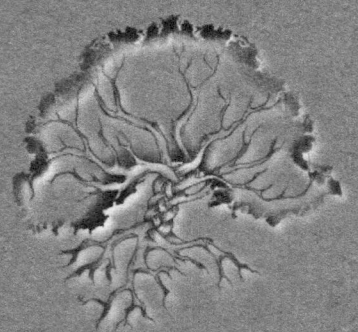

Thank You Lord

Week of: _____

 Teach Me

 Guide Me

 # Reflect

How has your faith grown over the years? Can you identify specific events that caused your faith to grow? How has your faith changed over the years? And how have you changed as a result of this?

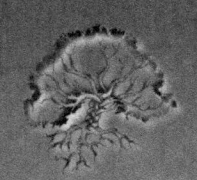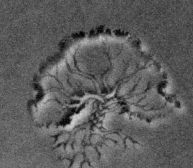

Future Generations

Highlights

My Prayers

LUKE 23:46

"WHEN JESUS HAD CRIED WITH A LOUD VOICE, HE SAID, FATHER, INTO THY HANDS I COMMEND MY SPIRIT: AND HAVING SAID THUS, HE GAVE UP THE GHOST".

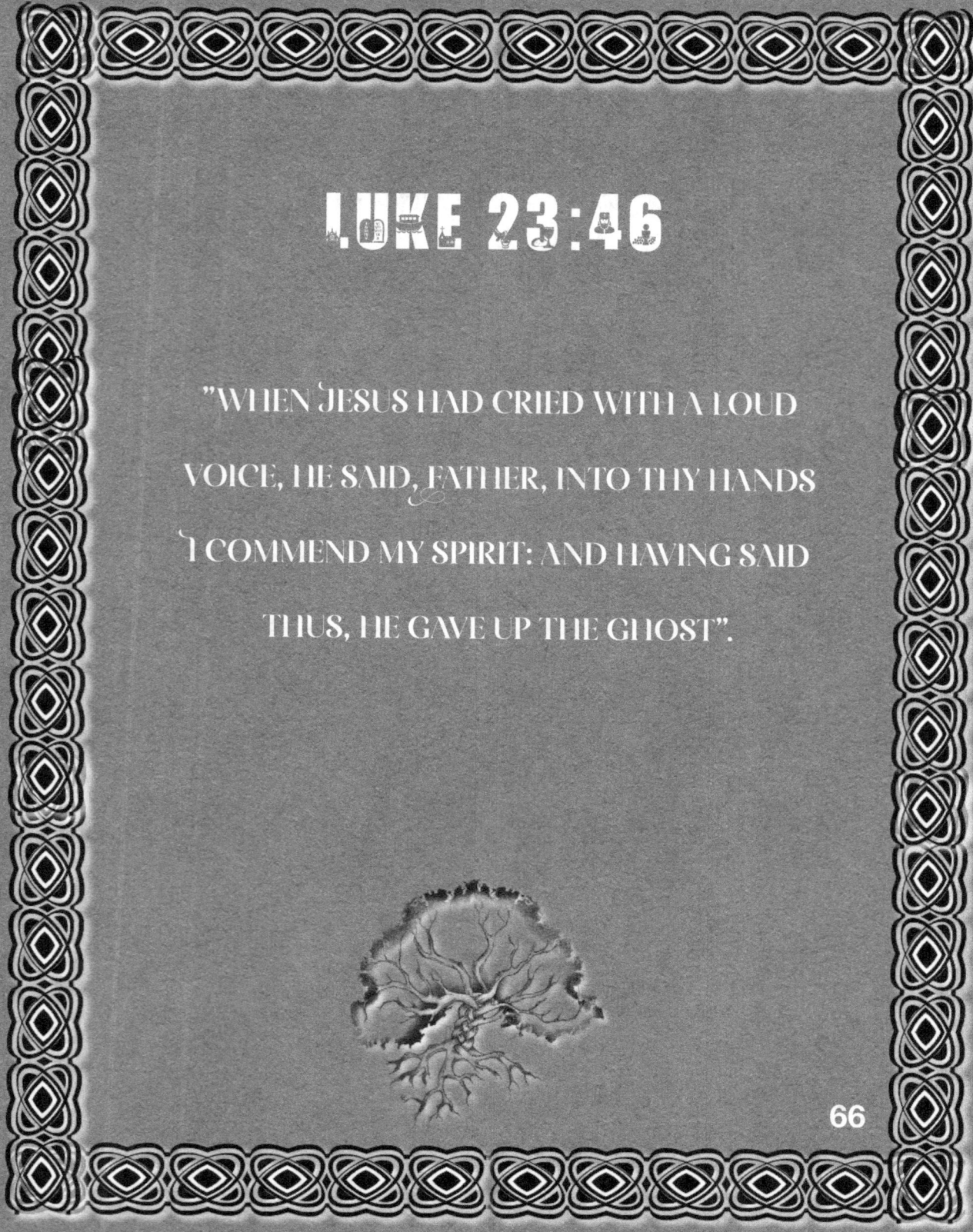

Thank You Lord

Week of: _____

 Teach Me

_____
_____
_____
_____
_____
_____
_____
_____
_____

 Guide Me

_____
_____
_____
_____
_____
_____
_____
_____
_____

 # Reflect

What is your favorite scripture passage is and

why?

_____

_____

_____

_____

_____

_____

_____

_____

_____

_____

_____

_____

_____

_____

_____

_____

_____

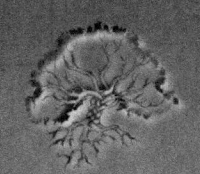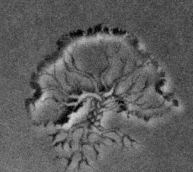

Future Generations

Highlights

My Prayers

DEUTERONOMY 31:8

"THE LORD, HE IT IS THAT DOTH GO BEFORE THEE; HE WILL BE WITH THEE, HE WILL NOT FAIL THEE, NEITHER FORSAKE THEE: FEAR NOT, NEITHER BE DISMAYED"

".

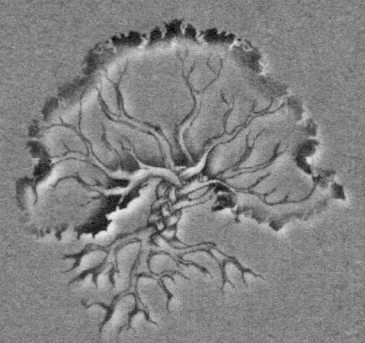

Thank You Lord

Week of: _____

 # Teach Me

_____
_____
_____
_____
_____
_____
_____
_____
_____
_____

 # Guide Me

_____
_____
_____
_____
_____
_____
_____
_____
_____
_____

 # Reflect

List all the things you believe about God. Pick

one to be your mantra for week

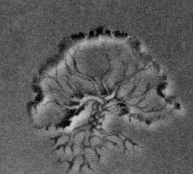

Future Generations

Highlights

My Prayers

JOHN 16:33

"GOD IS MY SALVATION; I WILL TRUST AND

NOT BE AFRAID. THE LORD, THE LORD

HIMSELF, IS MY STRENGTH AND MY DEFENSE;

HE HAS BECOME MY SALVATION"

"

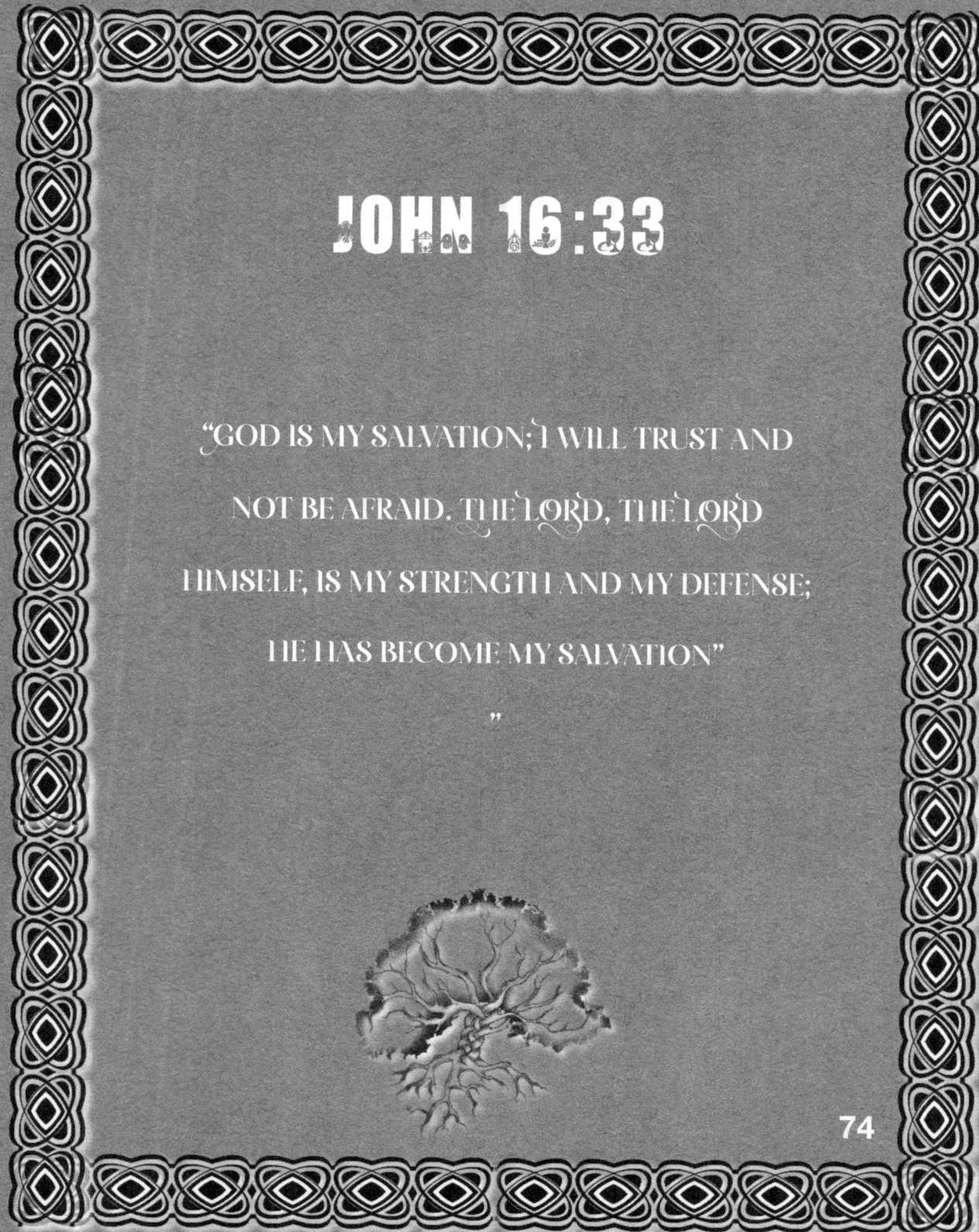

Thank You Lord

Week of: _____

 Teach Me

_____
_____
_____
_____
_____
_____
_____
_____
_____
_____
_____

 Guide Me

_____
_____
_____
_____
_____
_____
_____
_____
_____
_____

Reflect

Write about someone whose faith you admire and why.

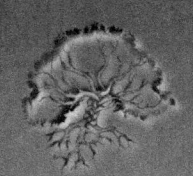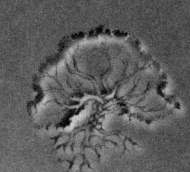

Future Generations

Highlights

My Prayers

ROMANS 15:13

"NOW THE GOD OF HOPE FILL YOU WITH ALL JOY AND PEACE IN BELIEVING, THAT YE MAY ABOUND IN HOPE, THROUGH THE POWER OF THE HOLY GHOST".

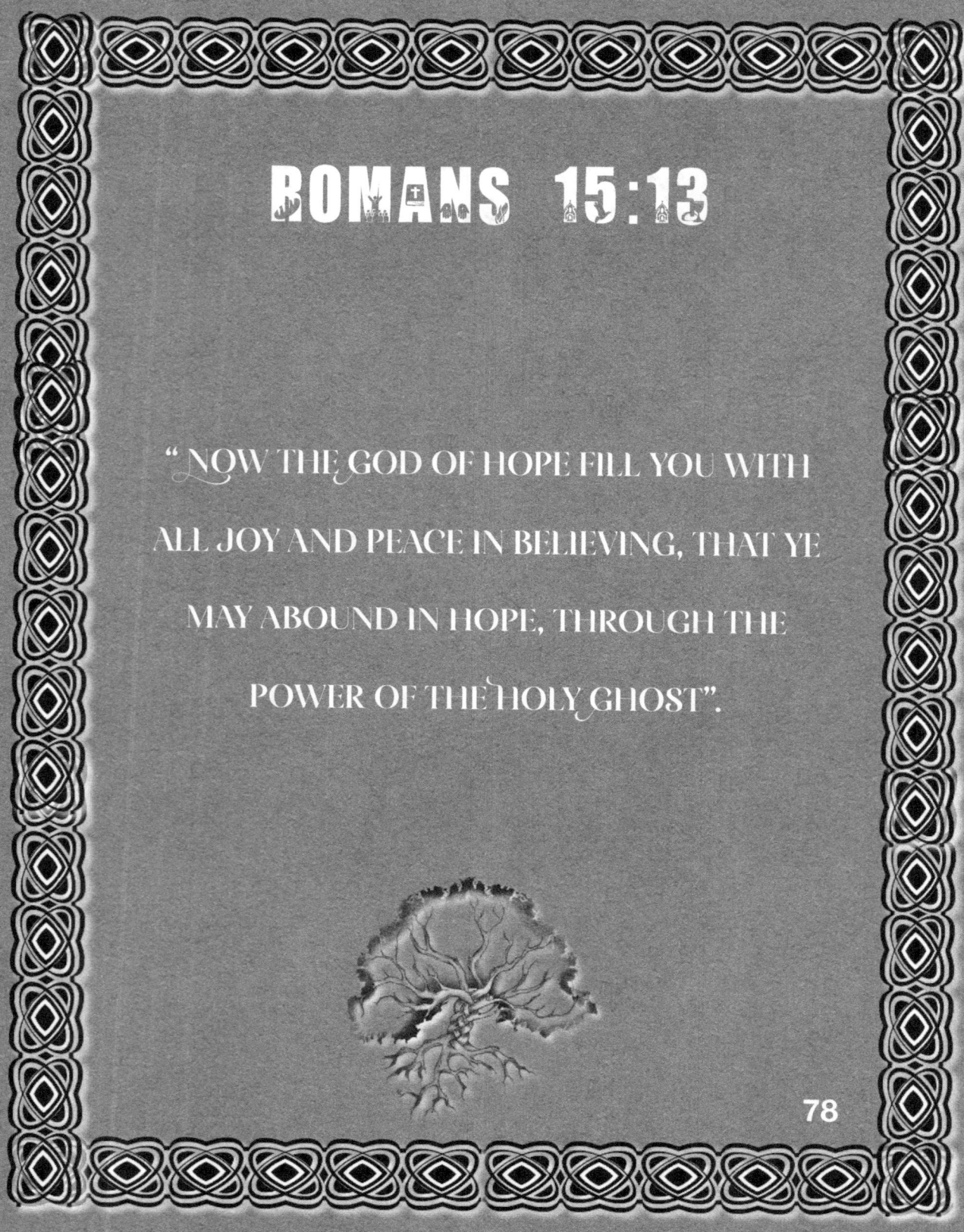

Thank You Lord

Week of: _____

 # Teach Me

_____
_____
_____
_____
_____
_____
_____
_____
_____
_____

 # Guide Me

_____
_____
_____
_____
_____
_____
_____
_____
_____
_____

 # Reflect

This week resolve to forgive. Write a letter to

someone you need to forgive offering forgiveness

to them

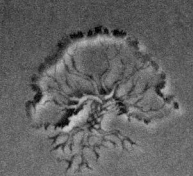

Future Generations

Highlights

My Prayers

JOHN 11:40

"JESUS SAITH UNTO HER, SAID I NOT UNTO THEE, THAT, IF THOU WOULDEST BELIEVE, THOU SHOULDEST SEE THE GLORY OF GOD?

".

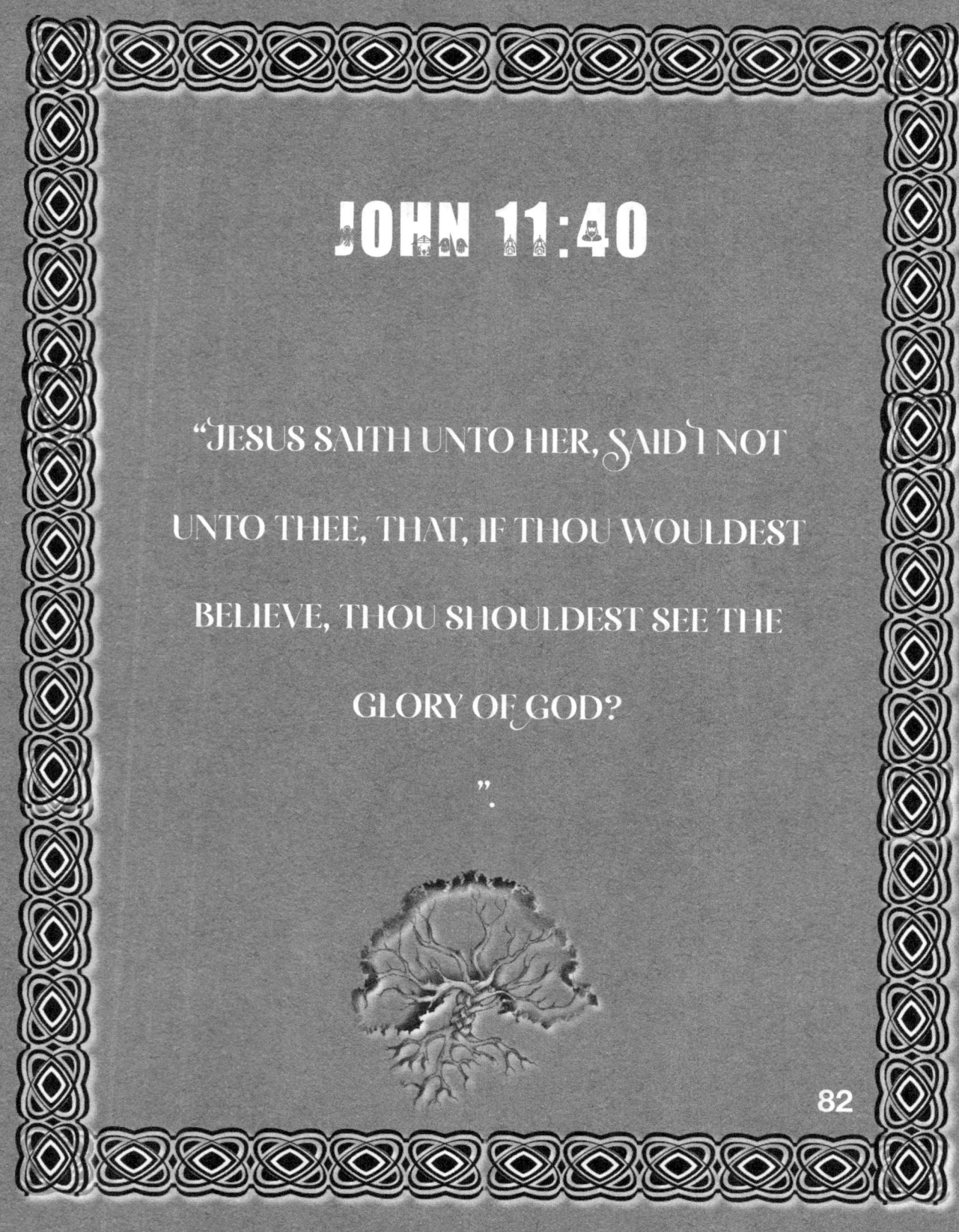

Thank You Lord

 Teach Me

Guide Me

 # Reflect

What things in nature can you use to prompt your

faith? Why have you chosen this symbol?

_____

_____

_____

_____

_____

_____

_____

_____

_____

_____

_____

_____

_____

_____

_____

_____

_____

_____

_____

_____

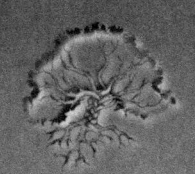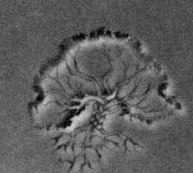

Future Generations

Highlights

My Prayers

PROVERBS 17:9

"HE THAT COVERETH A

TRANSGRESSION SEEKETH LOVE;

BUT HE THAT REPEATETH A

MATTER SEPARATETH VERY

FRIENDS"

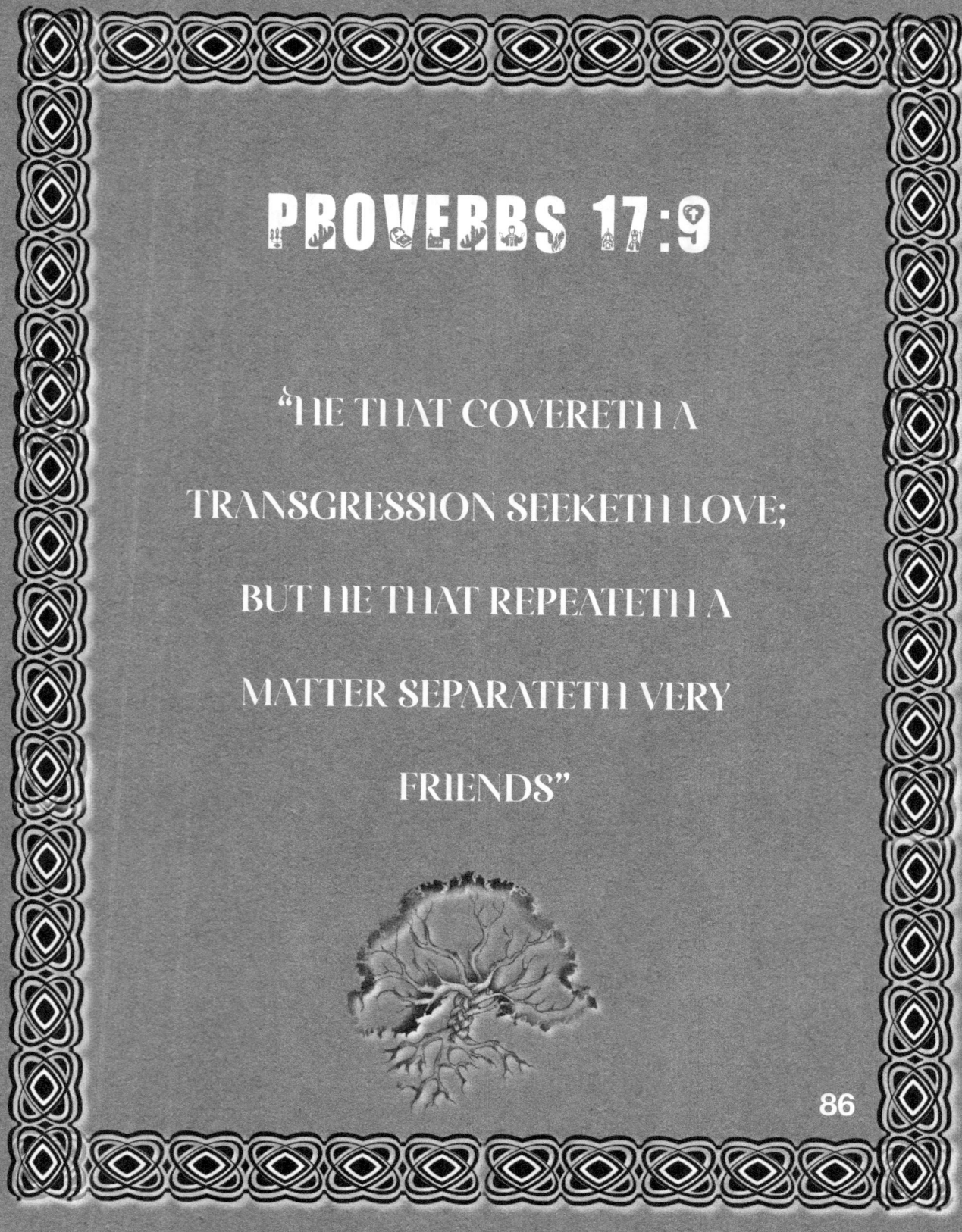

Thank You Lord

Week of: _____

 Teach Me

 Guide Me

 # Reflect

What do you see when you pray? How do you imagine God? Write a vivid picture of what you think God looks or feel like. Where are you? What do you smell, feel, taste, see?

_____
_____
_____
_____
_____
_____
_____
_____
_____
_____
_____
_____
_____
_____
_____
_____
_____
_____
_____
_____

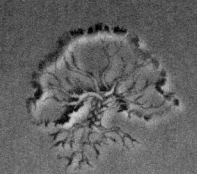
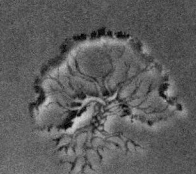

Future Generations

Highlights

My Prayers

COLOSSIANS 3:13

"FORBEARING ONE ANOTHER,

AND FORGIVING ONE ANOTHER,

IF ANY MAN HAVE A QUARREL

AGAINST ANY: EVEN AS CHRIST

FORGAVE YOU, SO ALSO DO YE".

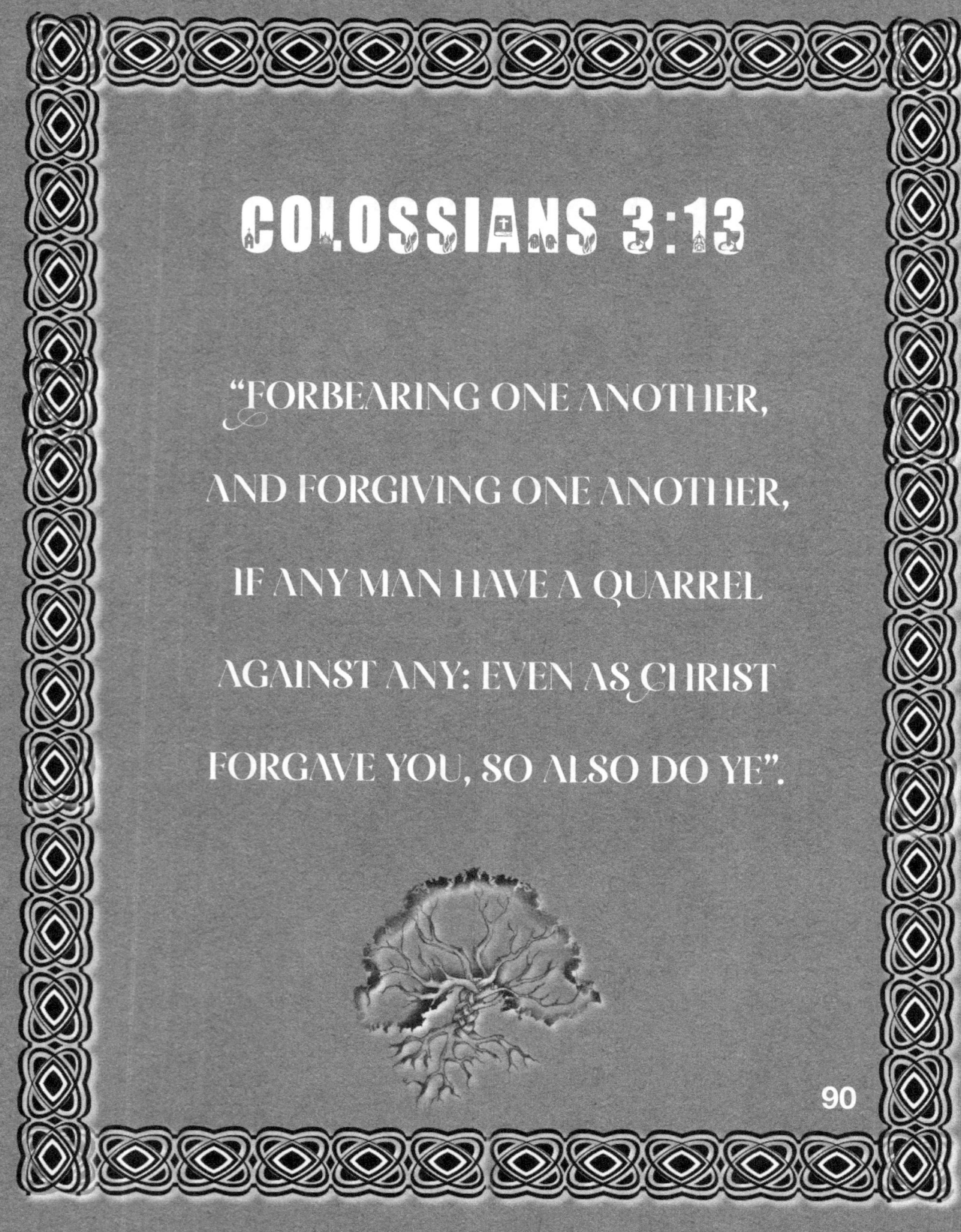

Thank You Lord

 Teach Me

_____
_____
_____
_____
_____
_____
_____
_____
_____
_____
_____
_____

Guide Me

_____
_____
_____
_____
_____
_____
_____
_____
_____

 # Reflect

What current stressors are impacting your faith?

_____
_____
_____
_____
_____
_____
_____
_____
_____
_____
_____
_____
_____
_____
_____
_____
_____
_____
_____

 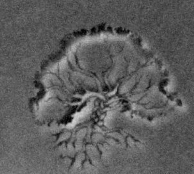

Future Generations

Highlights

My Prayers

ISAIAH 41:10

"FEAR THOU NOT; FOR I AM WITH THEE:

BE NOT DISMAYED; FOR I AM THY GOD:

I WILL STRENGTHEN THEE; YEA, I WILL HELP

THEE; YEA, I WILL UPHOLD THEE WITH THE

RIGHT HAND OF MY RIGHTEOUSNESS".

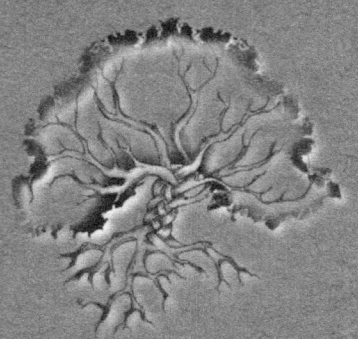

Thank You Lord

Week of: _____

 Teach Me

_____
_____
_____
_____
_____
_____
_____
_____
_____
_____
_____
_____

 Guide Me

_____
_____
_____
_____
_____
_____
_____
_____
_____

 # Reflect

With God all things are possible. What things are

possible for you with God by your side?

_____

_____

_____

_____

_____

_____

_____

_____

_____

_____

_____

_____

_____

_____

_____

_____

_____

_____

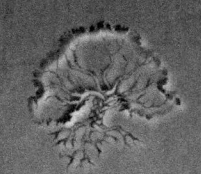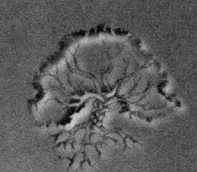

Future Generations

Highlights

My Prayers

PSALM 27:1

" THE LORD IS MY LIGHT AND MY

SALVATION;

WHOM SHALL I FEAR?

THE LORD IS THE STRENGTH OF MY LIFE;

OF WHOM SHALL I BE AFRAID?

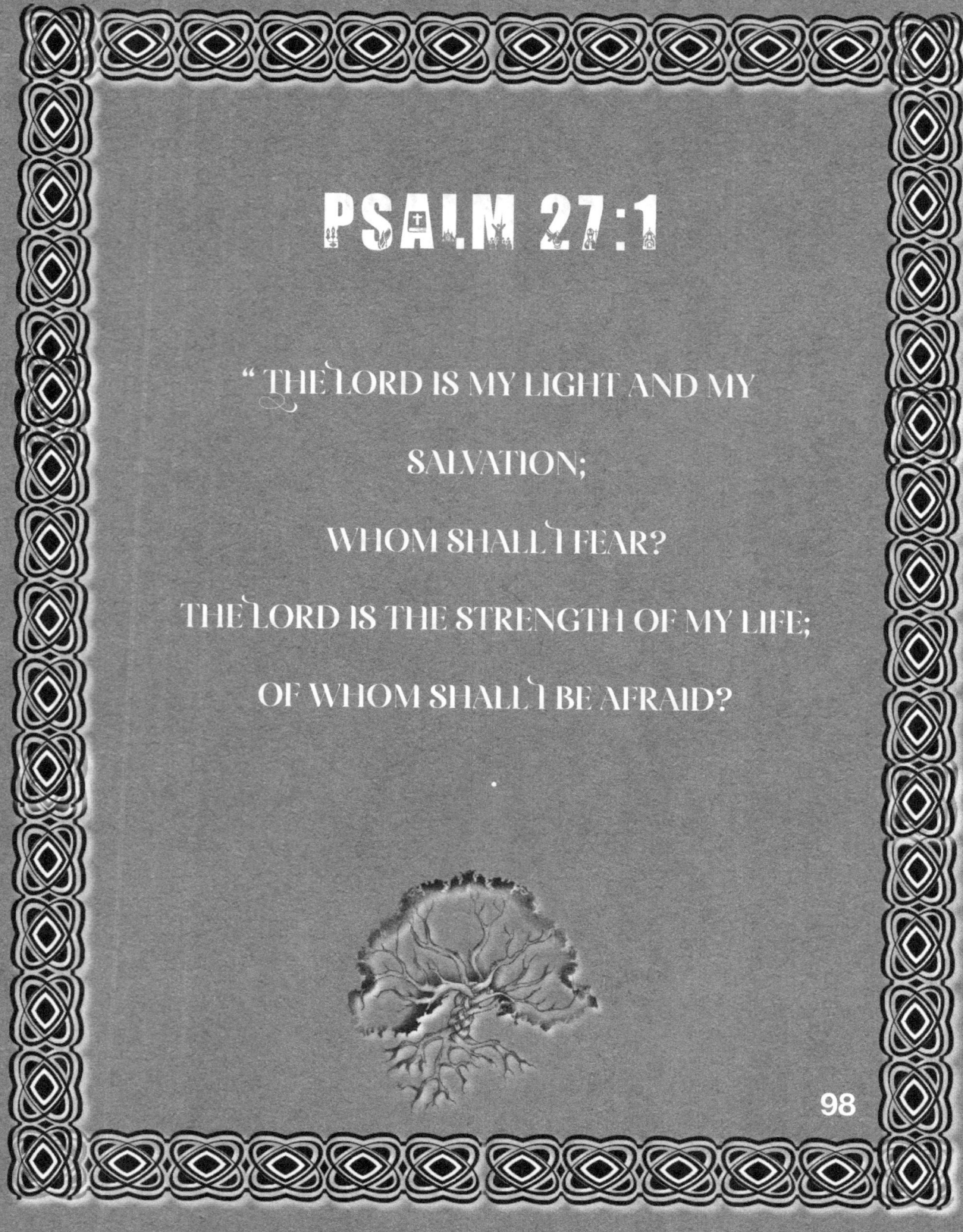

Thank You Lord

Week of: _____

 # Teach Me

_____
_____
_____
_____
_____
_____
_____
_____
_____
_____
_____

 # Guide Me

_____
_____
_____
_____
_____
_____
_____
_____

 # Reflect

Write out the lyrics of a song that encourages and

nurtures your faith.

_____

_____

_____

_____

_____

_____

_____

_____

_____

_____

_____

_____

_____

_____

_____

_____

_____

_____

_____

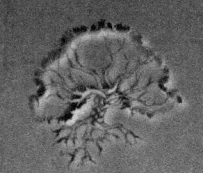

Future Generations

Highlights

My Prayers

1 JOHN 4:7

"BELOVED, LET US LOVE ONE ANOTHER: FOR LOVE IS OF GOD; AND EVERY ONE THAT LOVETH IS BORN OF GOD, AND KNOWETH GOD".

Thank You Lord

Week of: _____

 Teach Me

 Guide Me

 # Reflect

What is the connection between faith and

purpose?

_____
_____
_____
_____
_____
_____
_____
_____
_____
_____
_____
_____
_____
_____
_____
_____
_____
_____
_____

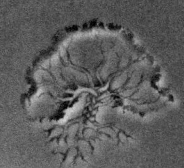

Future Generations

Highlights

My Prayers

1 JOHN 4:21

"AND THIS COMMANDMENT HAVE

WE FROM HIM, THAT HE WHO

LOVETH GOD LOVE HIS BROTHER

ALSO".

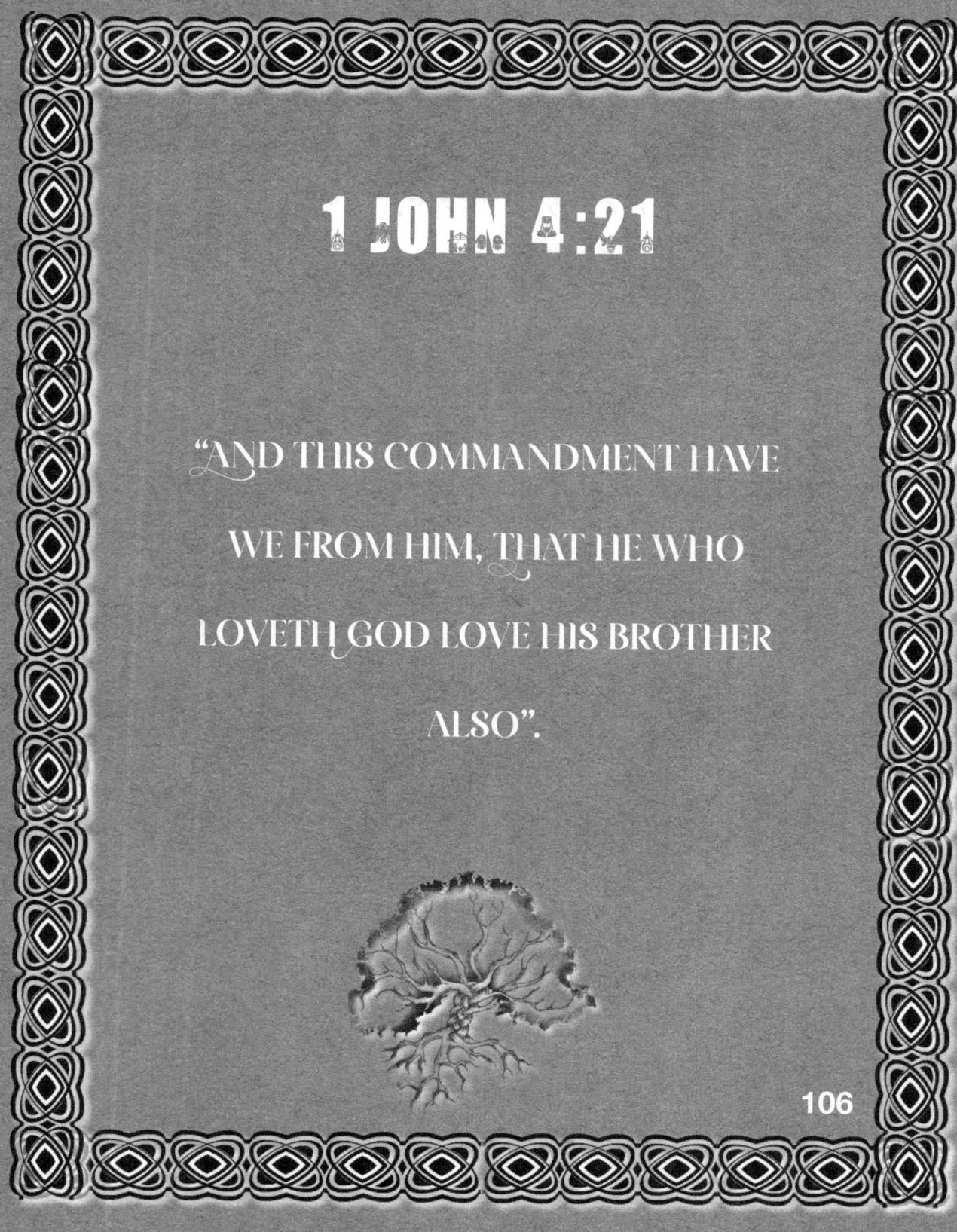

Thank You Lord

Week of: _____

 # Teach Me

_____
_____
_____
_____
_____
_____
_____
_____
_____
_____
_____

 # Guide Me

_____
_____
_____
_____
_____
_____
_____
_____
_____
_____
_____

 # Reflect

When you think of fear and doubt, which Bible character comes to mind? How did they overcome it? What can you learn from them?

_____
_____
_____
_____
_____
_____
_____
_____
_____
_____
_____
_____
_____
_____
_____
_____
_____
_____
_____
_____
_____

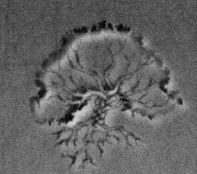 

Future Generations

Highlights

My Prayers

2 CORINTHIANS 9:7

"EVERY MAN ACCORDING AS HE PURPOSETH IN HIS HEART, SO LET HIM GIVE; NOT GRUDGINGLY, OR OF NECESSITY: FOR GOD LOVETH A CHEERFUL GIVER".

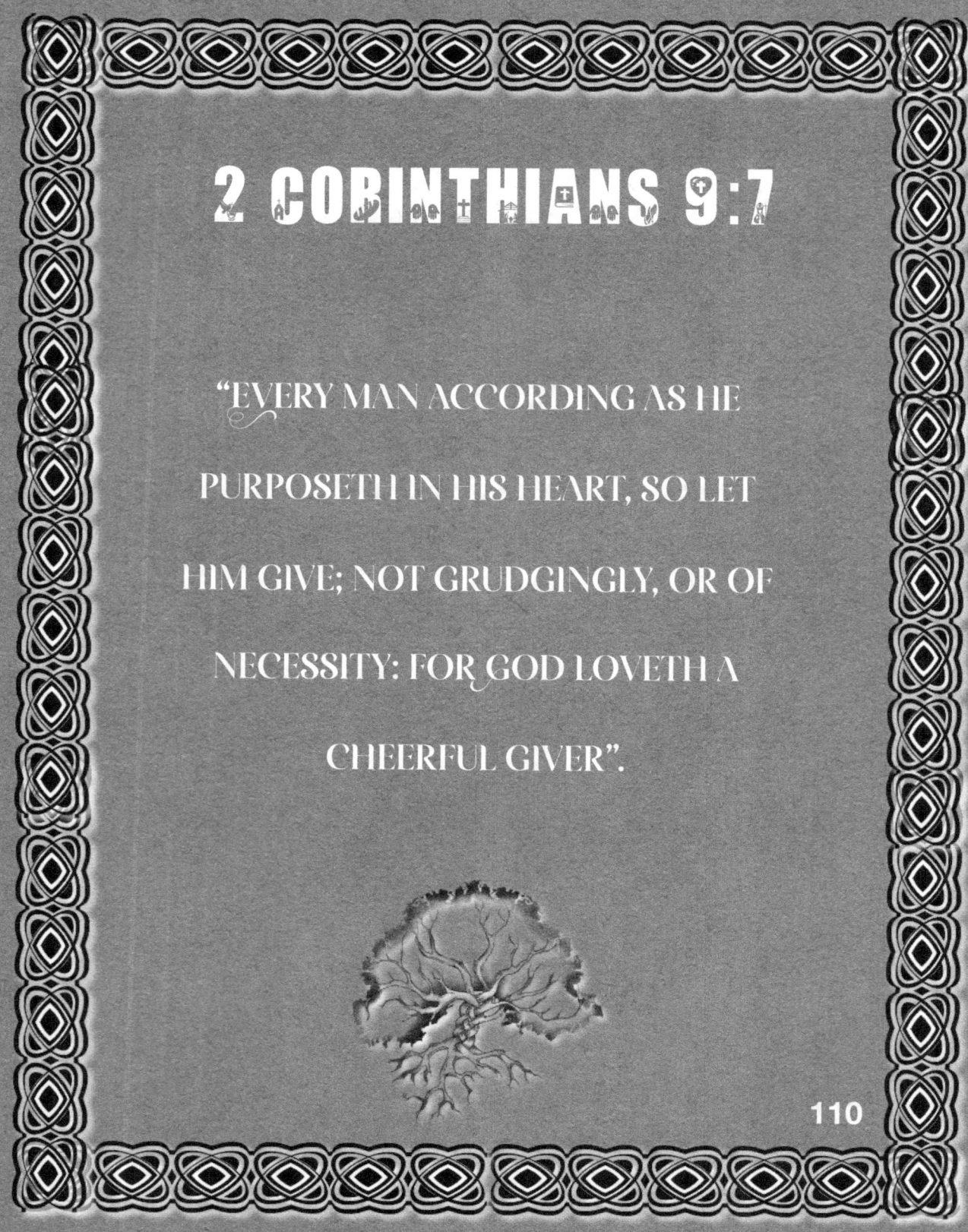

Reflect

Imagine you are in the crowd and Jesus is passing by. You cry out "Jesus, Son of God, have mercy on me." He stops, finds you in the crowd and say "What would you have me do?" What do you say to him?

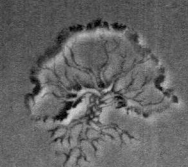
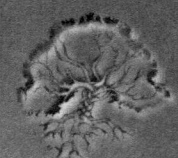

Future Generations

Highlights

My Prayers

JAMES 1:5

"IF ANY OF YOU LACK WISDOM, LET HIM ASK OF GOD, THAT GIVETH TO ALL MEN LIBERALLY, AND UPBRAIDETH NOT; AND IT SHALL BE GIVEN HIM".

Thank You Lord

Week of: _____

 # Teach Me

_____
_____
_____
_____
_____
_____
_____
_____
_____
_____
_____
_____
_____

 # Guide Me

_____
_____
_____
_____
_____
_____
_____
_____
_____
_____
_____
_____

 # Reflect

What is imposter syndrome? Can you identify a Bible character who struggled with it? How did they conquer it? What Biblical truth contradicts that lie?

_____
_____
_____
_____
_____
_____
_____
_____
_____
_____
_____
_____
_____
_____
_____
_____
_____
_____
_____
_____

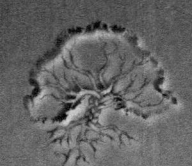

Future Generations

Highlights

My Prayers

JEREMIAH 29:10

"I HAVE FOR YOU"

DECLARES THE LORD

"PLANS TO PROSPER YOU

AND NOT TO HARM YOU.

PLANS TO GIVE YOU HOPE

AND A FUTURE".

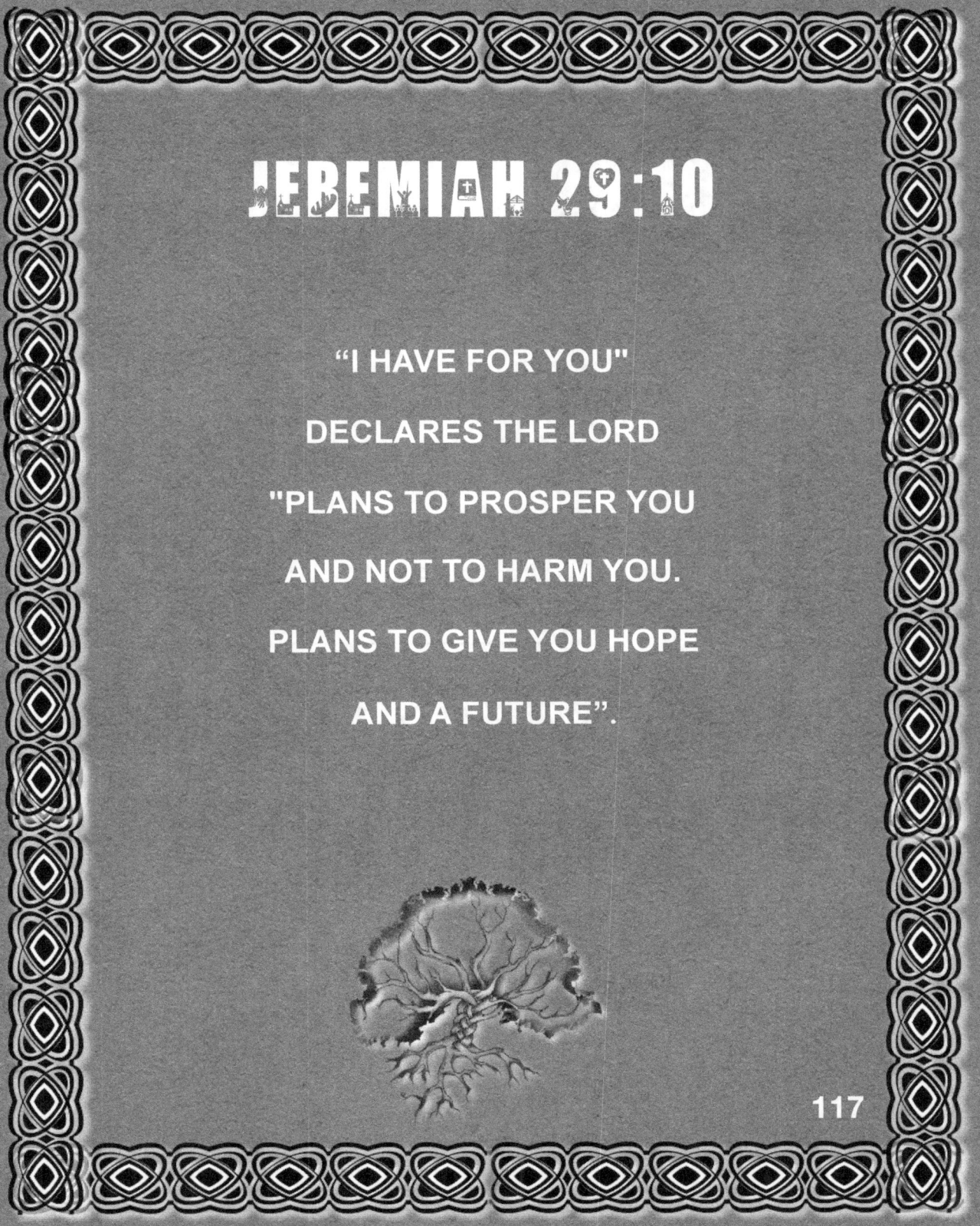

Thank You Lord

Teach Me

Guide Me

 # Reflect

> If you could choose *one* spiritual ideal to have right now, what would you want? (ie. patience, wisdom, empathy for others, knowing the right words to say to a friend, etc.) *Ask God for guidance.*

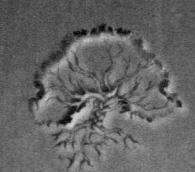
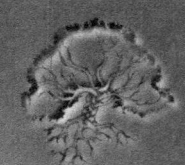

Future Generations

Highlights

My Prayers

PSALM 121:7-8

"THE LORD SHALL PRESERVE THEE FROM ALL EVIL HE SHALL PRESERVE THY SOUL.THE LORD SHALL PRESERVE THY GOING OUT AND THY COMING IN FROM THIS TIME FORTH, AND EVEN FOR EVERMORE"

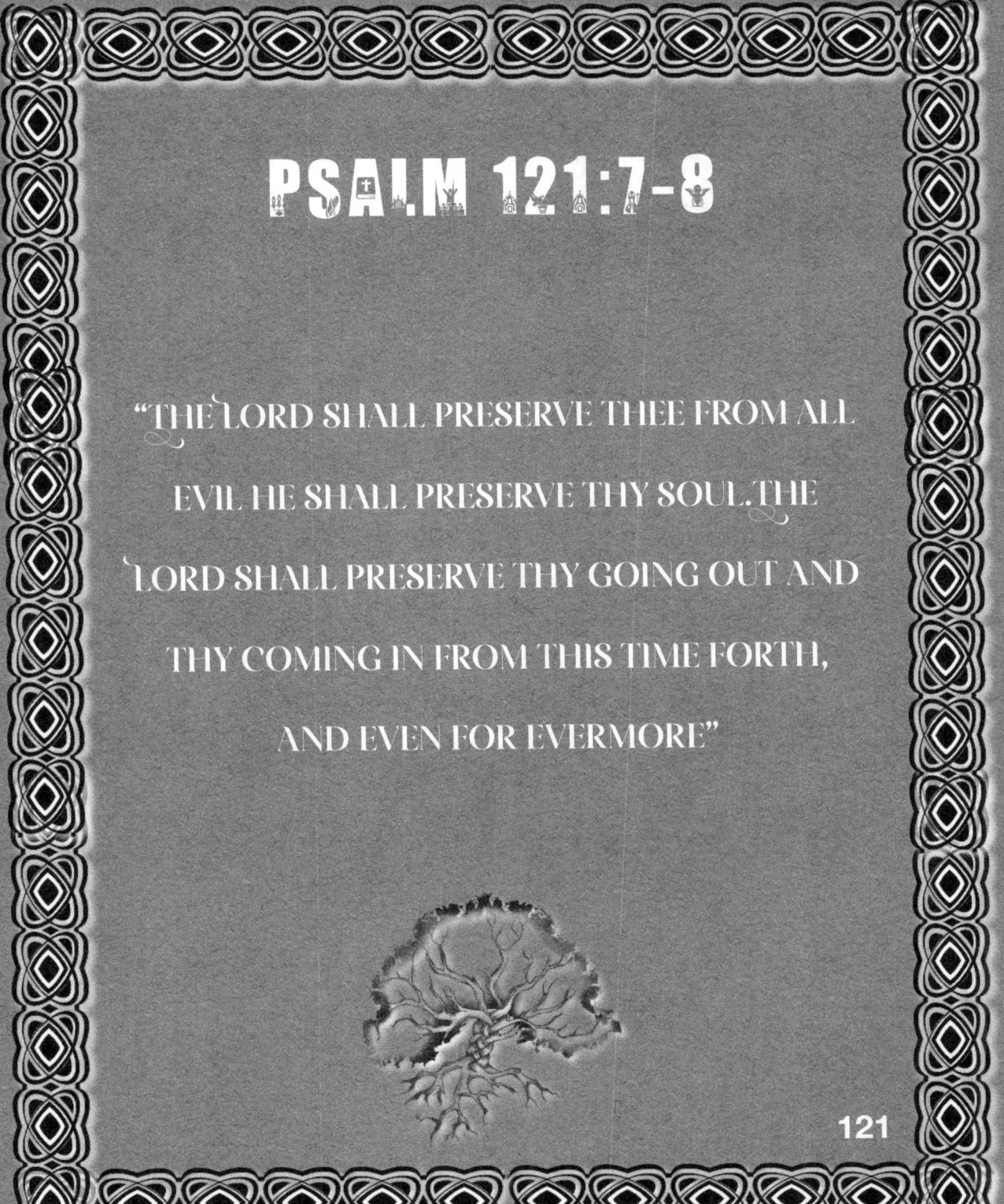

Thank You Lord

Week of: _____

 ♥ # Teach Me ♥

___

 ♥ # Guide Me ♥

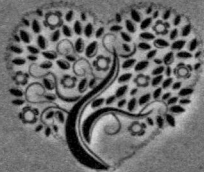

 # Reflect

How are you serving God on a daily basis? It doesn't have to be something big- it could be something as simple as cleaning the house so another person doesn't have to.

_____

_____

_____

_____

_____

_____

_____

_____

_____

_____

_____

_____

_____

_____

_____

_____

_____

_____

_____

_____

_____

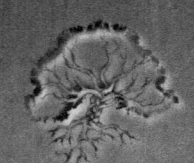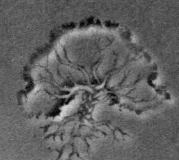

Future Generations

Highlights

My Prayers

DEUTERONOMY 4:39

"KNOW THEREFORE THIS DAY, AND

CONSIDER IT IN THINE HEART, THAT THE

LORD HE IS GOD IN HEAVEN ABOVE, AND

UPON THE EARTH BENEATH: THERE IS NONE

ELSE.

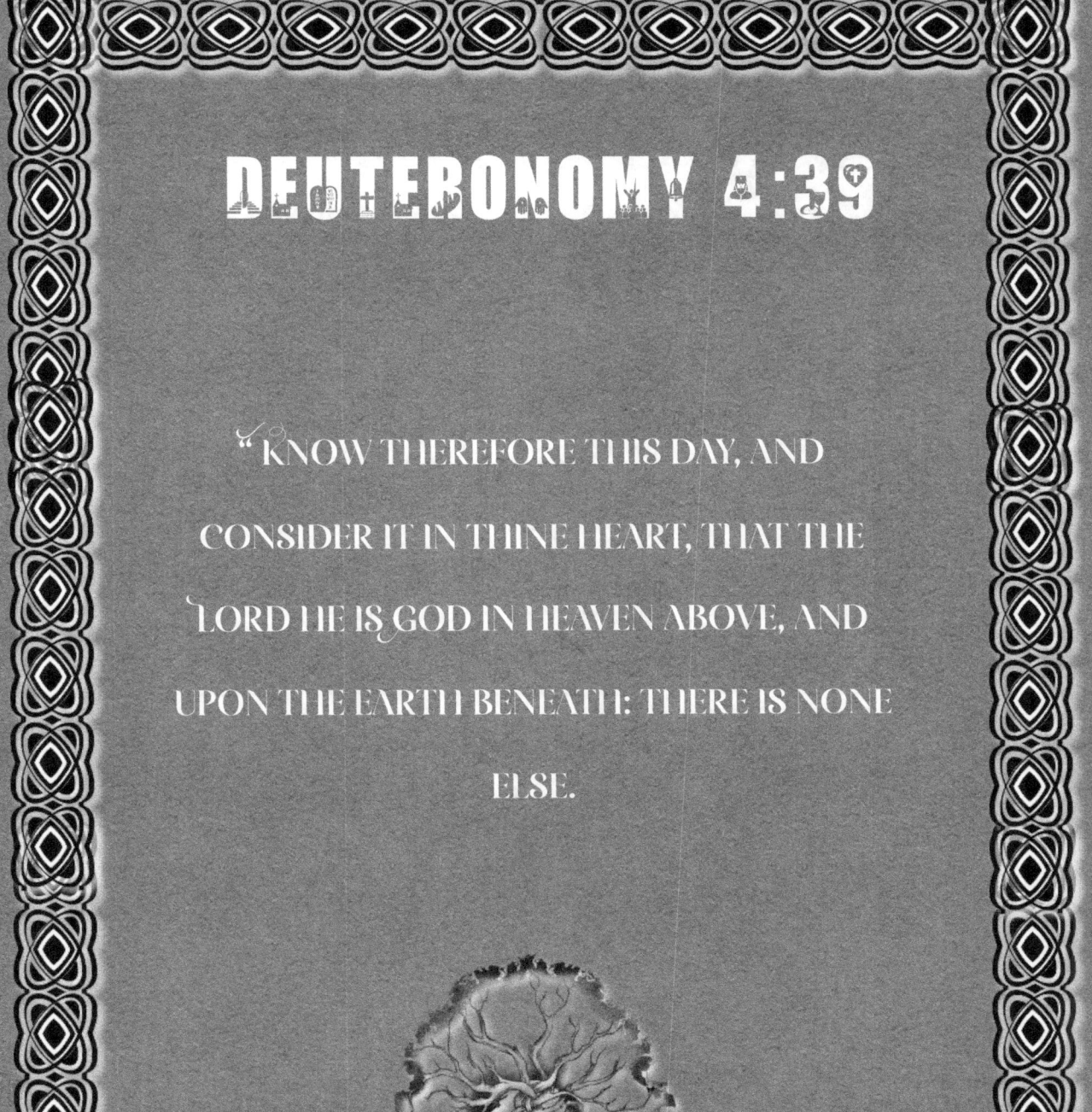

Thank You Lord

♥ # Teach Me ♥

♥ # Guide Me ♥

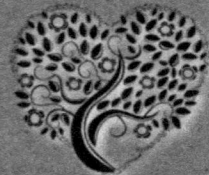

 # Reflect

Scripture says faith is a gift. How are you sure that you

have accepted that gift?

_____
_____
_____
_____
_____
_____
_____
_____
_____
_____
_____
_____
_____
_____
_____
_____
_____
_____
_____
_____
_____

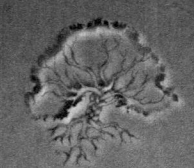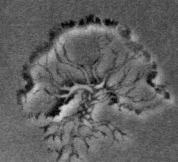

Future Generations

Highlights

My Prayers

JOHN 17:15

"I PRAY NOT THAT THOU SHOULDEST TAKE THEM OUT OF THE WORLD, BUT THAT THOU SHOULDEST KEEP THEM FROM THE EVIL".

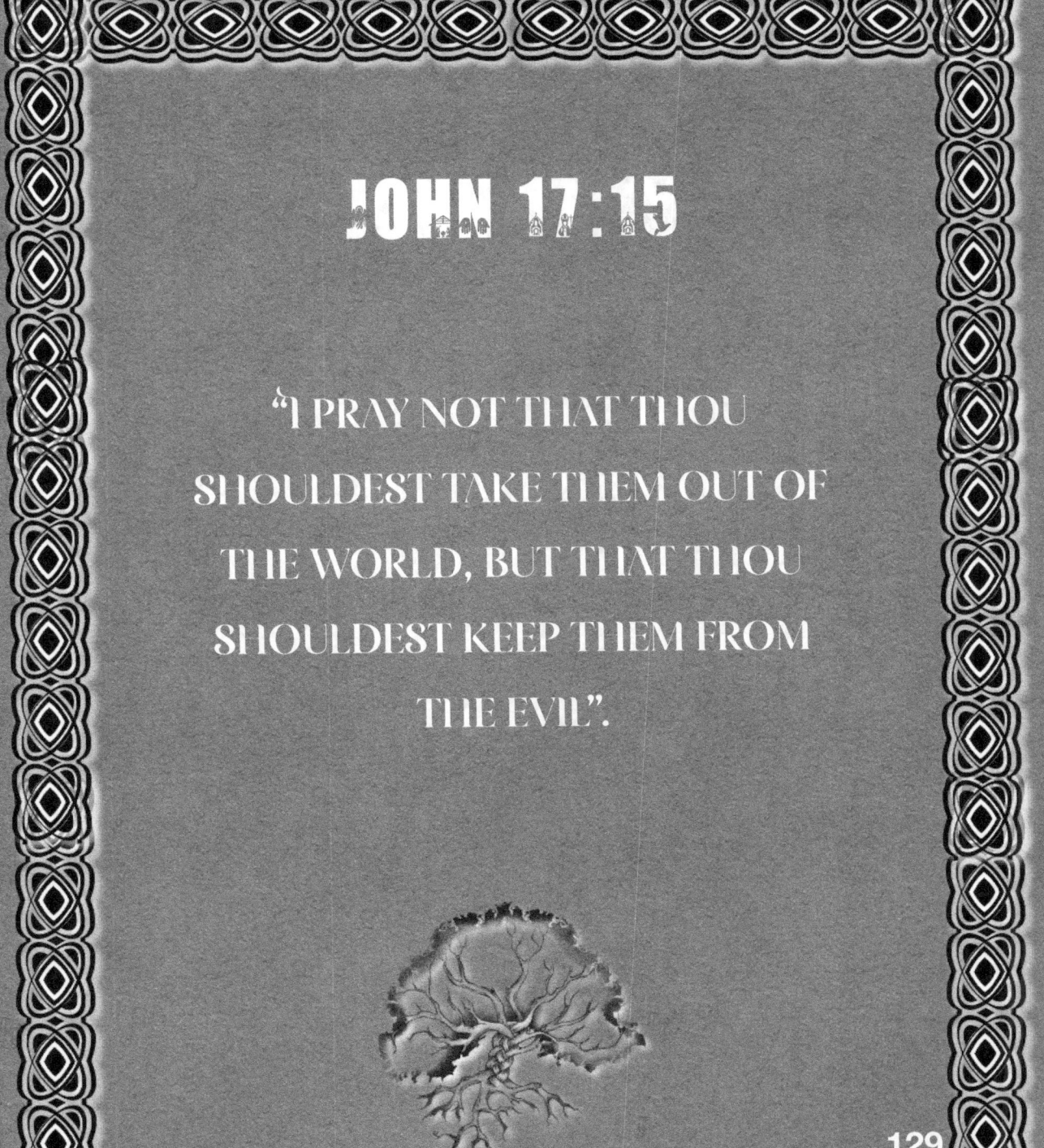

Thank You Lord

Week of: _____

 Teach Me

_____
_____
_____
_____
_____
_____
_____
_____
_____
_____

 Guide Me

_____
_____
_____
_____
_____
_____
_____
_____

 # Reflect

Think of one person you could help with their faith. What specific thing can you do for or with them?

_____
_____
_____
_____
_____
_____
_____
_____
_____
_____
_____
_____
_____
_____
_____
_____
_____
_____
_____
_____
_____
_____
_____
_____

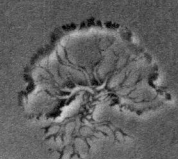

Future Generations

Highlights

My Prayers

1 THESSALONIANS 5:16-18

"REJOICE EVERMORE. PRAY WITHOUT CEASING. IN EVERY THING GIVE THANKS: FOR THIS IS THE WILL OF GOD IN CHRIST JESUS CONCERNING YOU".

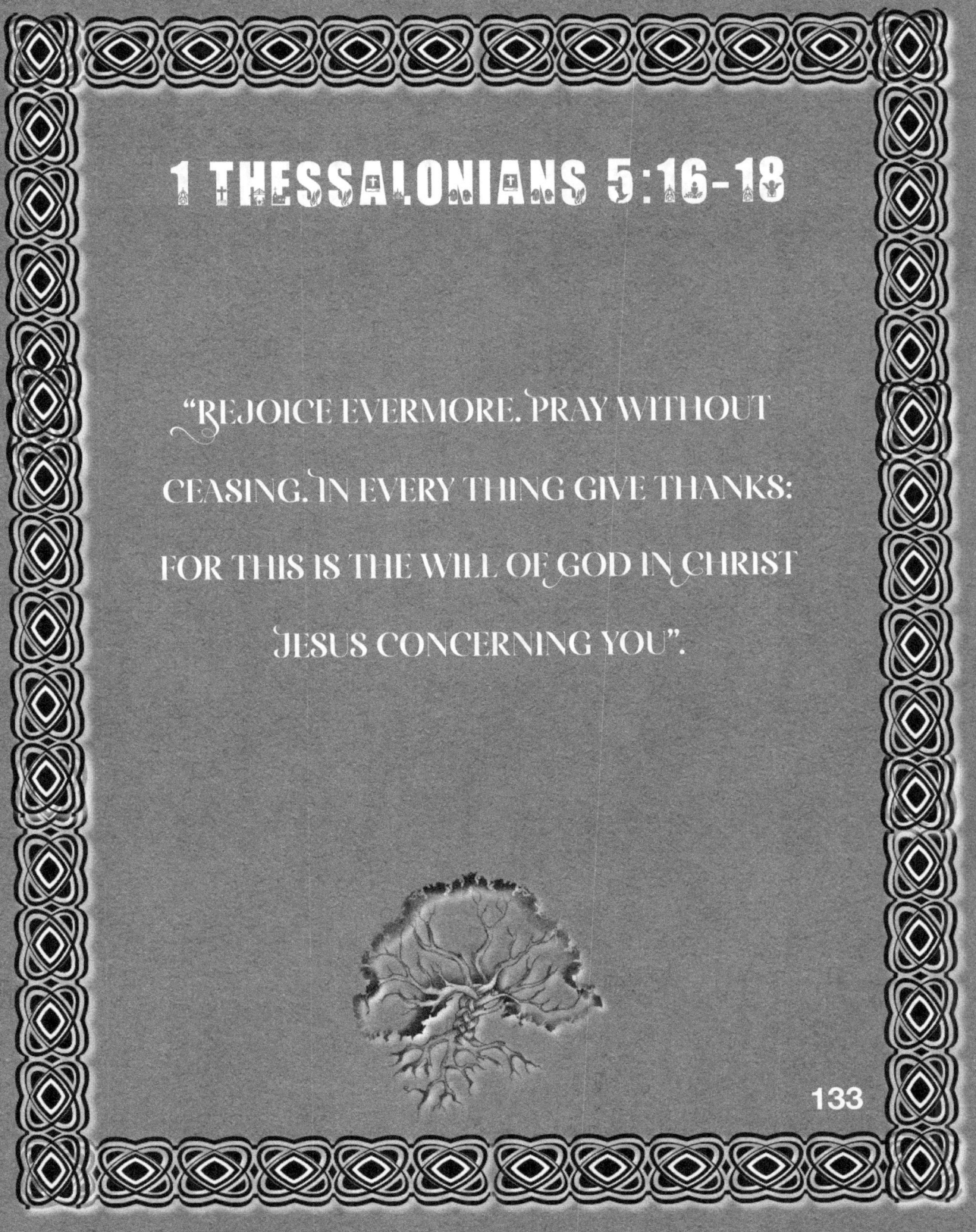

Thank You Lord

Week of: _____

 Teach Me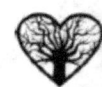

_____
_____
_____
_____
_____
_____
_____
_____
_____

 Guide Me

_____
_____
_____
_____
_____
_____
_____
_____
_____
_____

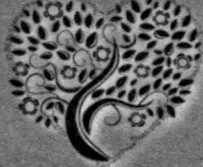

 # Reflect

What are 10 things that God has blessed you with? Try not to

think of the obvious things like good health and money for food.

Try to find the small pleasures that are often missed.

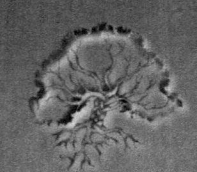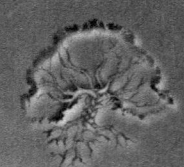

Future Generations

Highlights

My Prayers

PSALM 16:11

"REJOICE EVERMORE. PRAY WITHOUT CEASING. IN EVERY THING GIVE THANKS: FOR THIS IS THE WILL OF GOD IN CHRIST JESUS CONCERNING YOU.

Thank You Lord

Week of: _____

 # Teach Me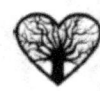

_____
_____
_____
_____
_____
_____
_____
_____
_____
_____
_____

 # Guide Me

_____
_____
_____
_____
_____
_____
_____
_____
_____
_____

 # Reflect

Was there a time recently when you wish you had gone to God first but didn't? What could you do differently next time so that you go to him first?

_____
_____
_____
_____
_____
_____
_____
_____
_____
_____
_____
_____
_____
_____
_____
_____
_____
_____
_____
_____
_____
_____

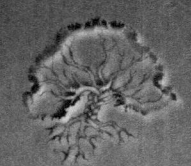
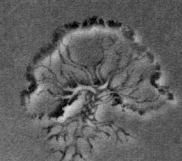

Future Generations

Highlights

My Prayers

ROMANS 6:15

"WHAT THEN? SHALL WE SIN, BECAUSE WE ARE
NOT UNDER THE LAW, BUT UNDER GRACE? GOD
FORBID"

Thank You Lord

Week of: _____

 Teach Me

_____
_____
_____
_____
_____
_____
_____
_____
_____
_____

 Guide Me

_____
_____
_____
_____
_____
_____
_____
_____
_____

 # Reflect

Think of something bad that happened to you recently.

Consider five ways that God might use that bad thing for

something good.

_____
_____
_____
_____
_____
_____
_____
_____
_____
_____
_____
_____
_____
_____
_____
_____
_____
_____
_____
_____
_____
_____
_____

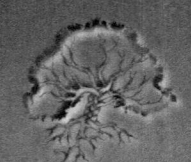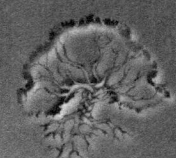

Future Generations

Highlights

My Prayers

1 CORINTHIANS 10:23

"ALL THINGS ARE LAWFUL FOR ME, BUT ALL THINGS ARE NOT EXPEDIENT: ALL THINGS ARE LAWFUL FOR ME, BUT ALL THINGS EDIFY NOT".

Thank You Lord

Week of: _____

 # Teach Me

_____
_____
_____
_____
_____
_____
_____
_____
_____
_____

 # Guide Me

_____
_____
_____
_____
_____
_____
_____
_____
_____
_____
_____

 # Reflect

If you could come up with *one word* that would sum up this

season of your life, what would it be? Why did you choose that

word?

_____

_____

_____

_____

_____

_____

_____

_____

_____

_____

_____

_____

_____

_____

_____

_____

_____

_____

_____

_____

_____

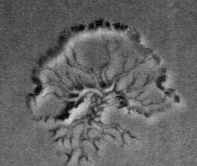

Future Generations

Highlights

My Prayers

HEBREWS 4:16

"LET US THEREFORE COME BOLDLY UNTO THE
THRONE OF GRACE, THAT WE MAY OBTAIN
MERCY, AND FIND GRACE TO HELP IN TIME OF
NEED.".

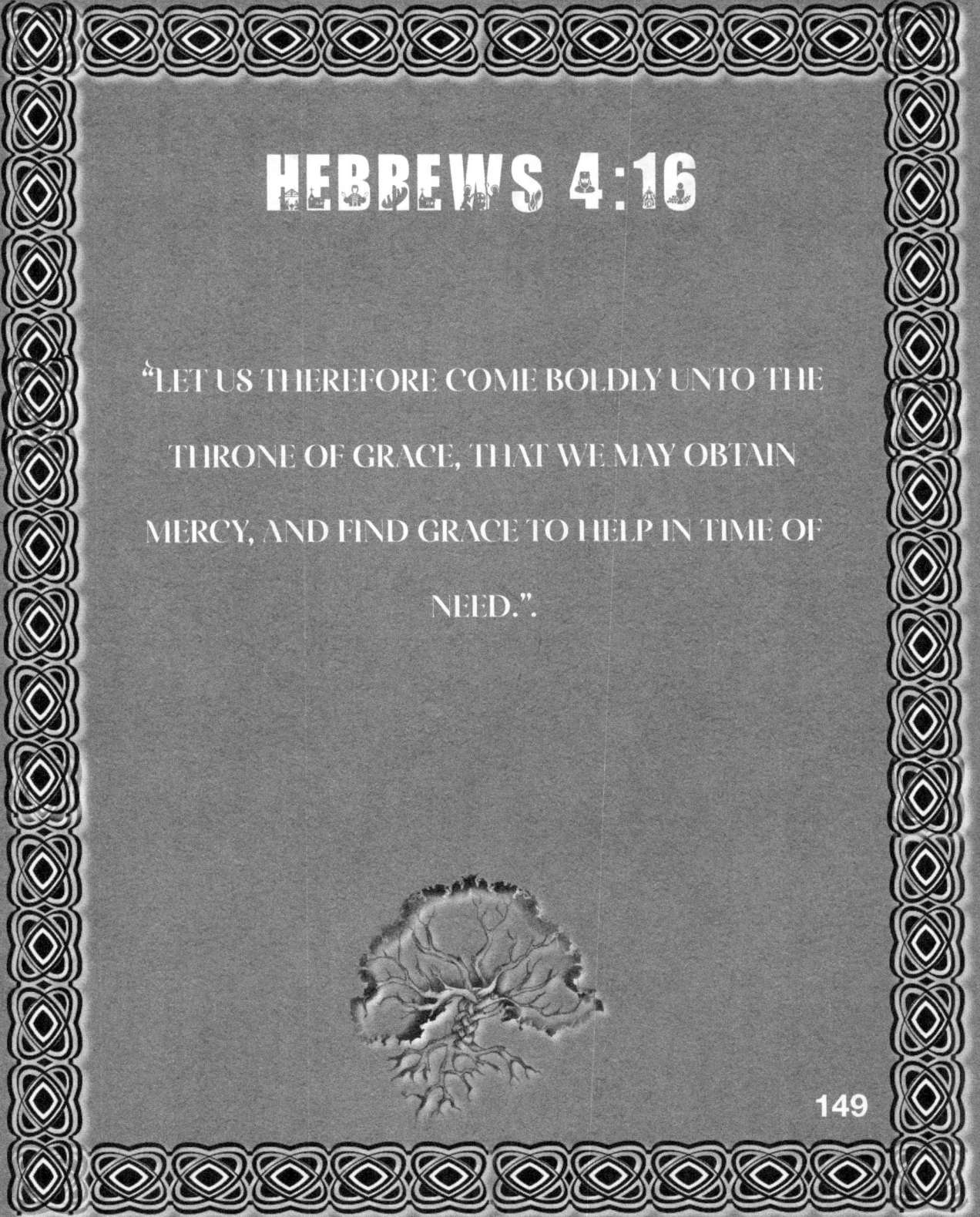

Thank You Lord

Week of: _____

 Teach Me

_____
_____
_____
_____
_____
_____
_____
_____
_____

 Guide Me

_____
_____
_____
_____
_____
_____
_____
_____

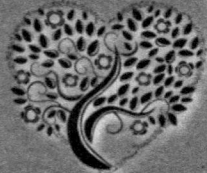

 # Reflect

Think of a song, a movie, or an event that has encouraged you recently. Why do you think it spoke to you? What do you think God is trying to tell you?

_____

_____

_____

_____

_____

_____

_____

_____

_____

_____

_____

_____

_____

_____

_____

_____

_____

_____

_____

_____

_____

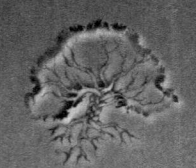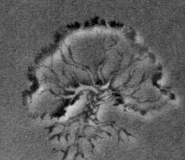

Future Generations

Highlights

My Prayers

EPHESIANS 2:4-5

"GOD, WHO IS RICH IN MERCY, FOR HIS GREAT LOVE WHEREWITH HE LOVED US, EVEN WHEN WE WERE DEAD IN SINS, HATH QUICKENED US TOGETHER WITH CHRIST, (BY GRACE YE ARE SAVED).".

Thank You Lord

Week of: _____

 ## Teach Me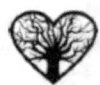

_____
_____
_____
_____
_____
_____
_____
_____
_____

Guide Me

_____
_____
_____
_____
_____
_____
_____
_____

 # Reflect

What are some lies you have been believing lately about your own life? Find a Bible verse that corrects these lies and reminds you of the truth.

_____
_____
_____
_____
_____
_____
_____
_____
_____
_____
_____
_____
_____
_____
_____
_____
_____
_____
_____
_____
_____

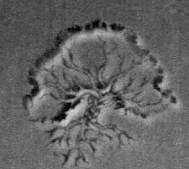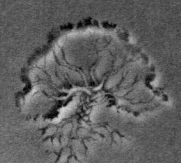

Future Generations

Highlights

My Prayers

MARK 12:31

"THE SECOND IS LIKE, NAMELY THIS, THOU SHALT LOVE THY NEIGHBOR AS THYSELF. THERE IS NONE OTHER COMMANDMENT GREATER THAN THESE".

Thank You Lord

Week of: _____

 # Teach Me

_____
_____
_____
_____
_____
_____
_____
_____
_____
_____
_____

Guide Me

_____
_____
_____
_____
_____
_____
_____
_____
_____
_____
_____
_____

 # Reflect

What past childhood trauma is affecting your faith

now?

_____
_____
_____
_____
_____
_____
_____
_____
_____
_____
_____
_____
_____
_____
_____
_____
_____
_____
_____
_____
_____
_____
_____
_____
_____
_____

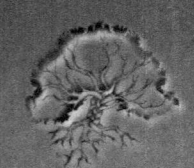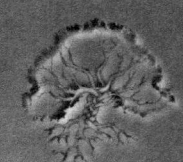

Future Generations

Highlights

My Prayers

1 PETER 3:8

"FINALLY, BE YE ALL OF ONE MIND, HAVING

COMPASSION ONE OF ANOTHER, LOVE AS

BRETHREN, BE PITIFUL, BE COURTEOUS".

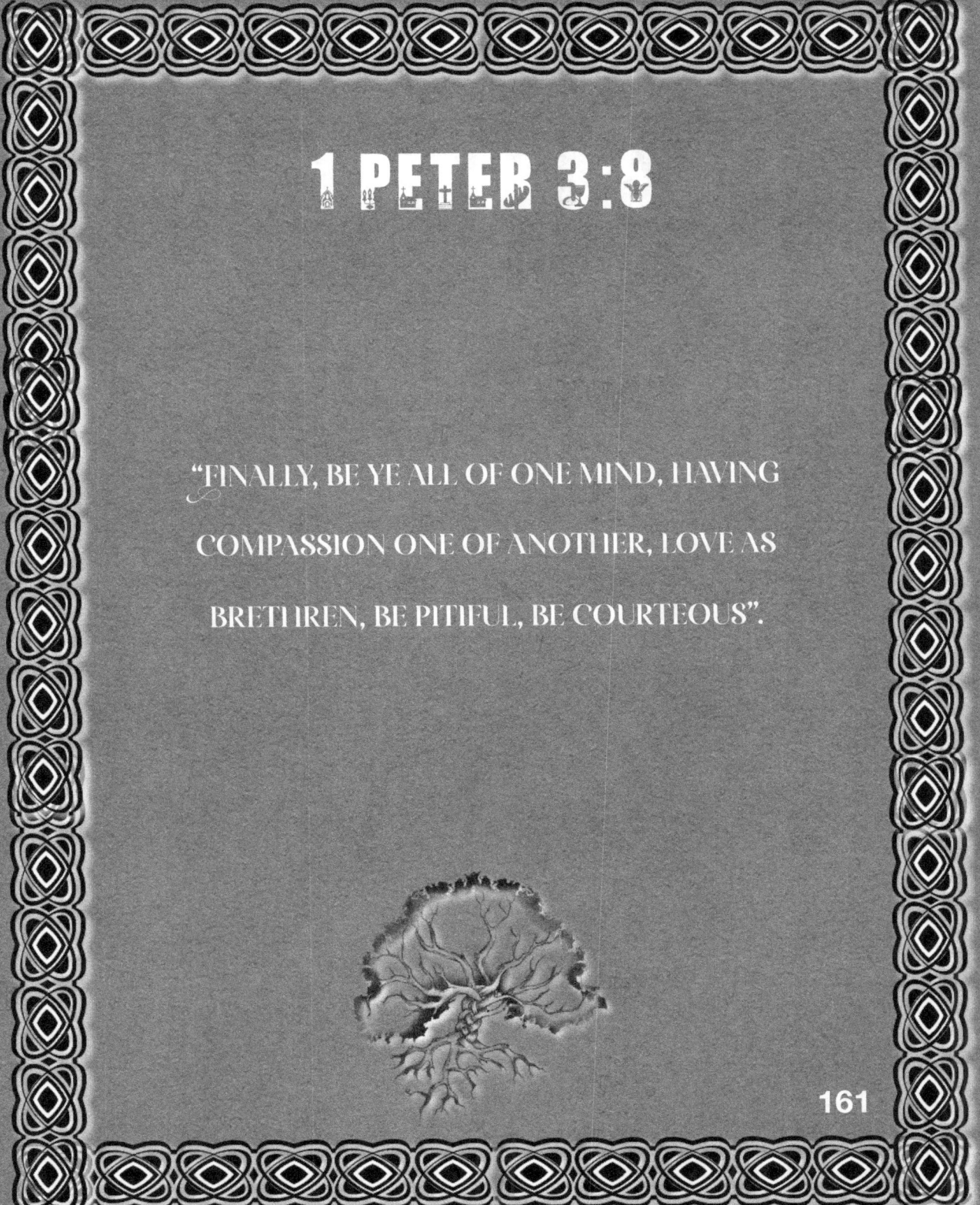

Thank You Lord

 # Teach Me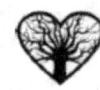

 # Guide Me

 # Reflect

What's your current body image? Do you feel confident that
your physical health habits will allow you to be a vessel for the
Holy Spirit?

_____
_____
_____
_____
_____
_____
_____
_____
_____
_____
_____
_____
_____
_____
_____
_____
_____
_____
_____
_____
_____
_____
_____
_____

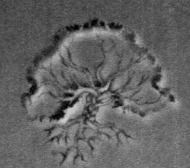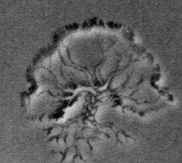

Future Generations

Highlights

My Prayers

PROVERBS 6:20

" MY SON, KEEP THY FATHER'S

COMMANDMENT,

AND FORSAKE NOT THE LAW OF THY

MOTHER".

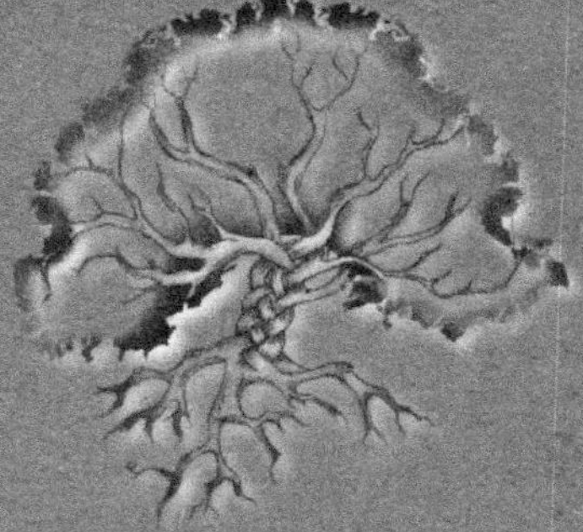

Thank You Lord

Week of: _____

 **Teach Me**

_____
_____
_____
_____
_____
_____
_____
_____
_____

Guide Me

_____
_____
_____
_____
_____
_____
_____
_____
_____
_____

 # Reflect

What is something happening right now that you can't

accomplish without God's help?

_____

_____

_____

_____

_____

_____

_____

_____

_____

_____

_____

_____

_____

_____

_____

_____

_____

_____

_____

_____

_____

_____

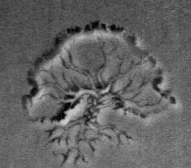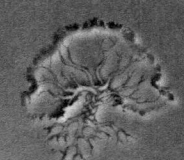

Future Generations

Highlights

My Prayers

PROVERBS 10:17

"HE IS IN THE WAY OF LIFE THAT KEEPETH

INSTRUCTION:

BUT HE THAT REFUSETH REPROOF ERRETH".

169

Thank You Lord

Week of: _____

 Teach Me

_____
_____
_____
_____
_____
_____
_____
_____
_____
_____

 Guide Me

_____
_____
_____
_____
_____
_____
_____
_____
_____
_____

 # Reflect

Think of a time in your life when you thought God had left you
alone. Looking back, do you see what he was doing to help you
in this season?

_____
_____
_____
_____
_____
_____
_____
_____
_____
_____
_____
_____
_____
_____
_____
_____
_____
_____
_____
_____
_____
_____
_____

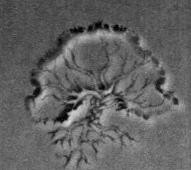

Future Generations

Highlights

My Prayers

PROVERBS 14:29

"HE THAT IS SLOW TO WRATH IS OF GREAT

UNDERSTANDING:BUT HE THAT IS HASTY OF

SPIRIT EXALTETH FOLLY".

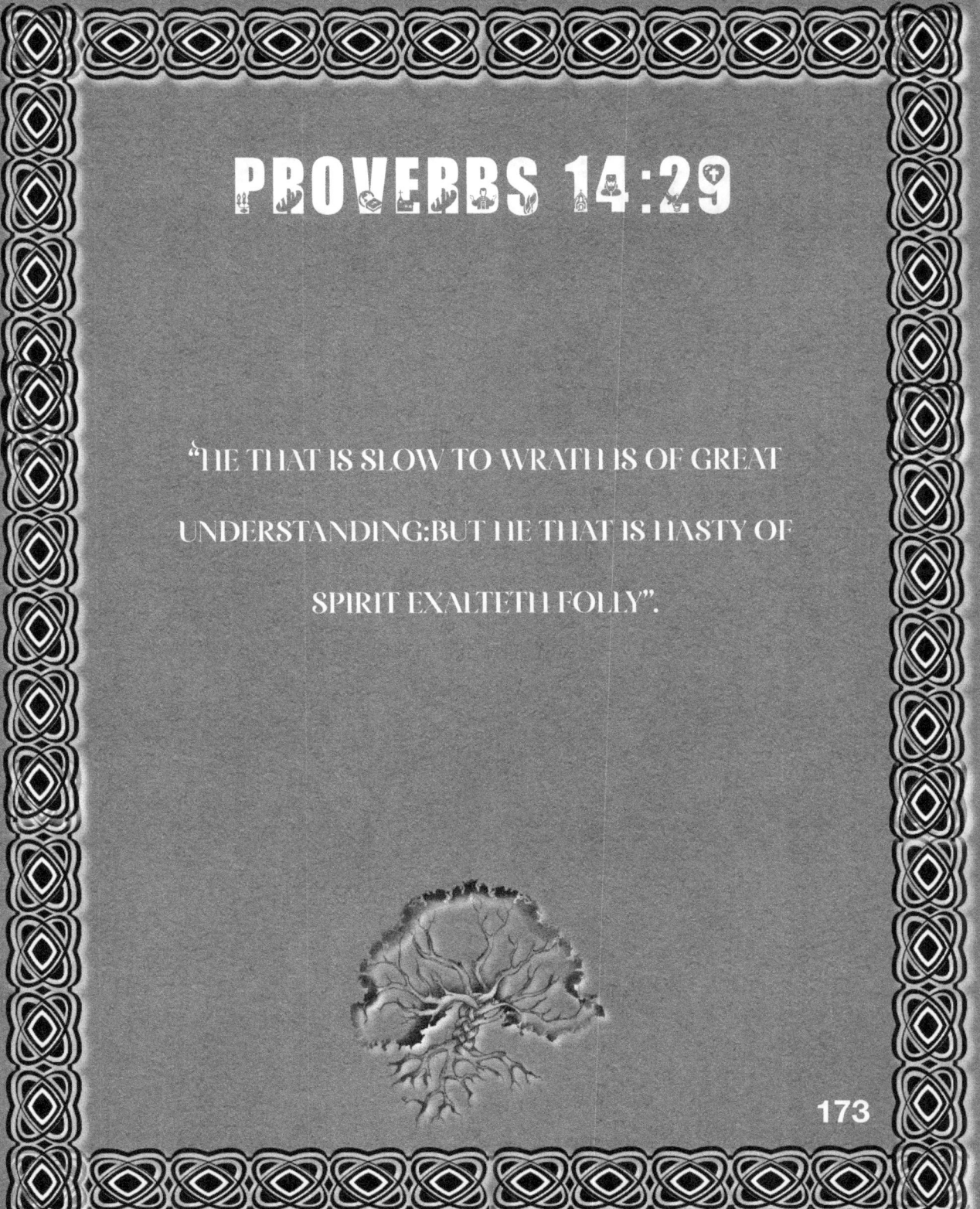

Thank You Lord

Week of: _____

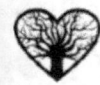 # Teach Me

_____
_____
_____
_____
_____
_____
_____
_____

Guide Me

_____
_____
_____
_____
_____
_____
_____

 # Reflect

Do you think faith and logic have anything to do with each other? What Bible verses can you use to support your thoughts?

_____
_____
_____
_____
_____
_____
_____
_____
_____
_____
_____
_____
_____
_____
_____
_____
_____
_____
_____
_____
_____
_____
_____
_____

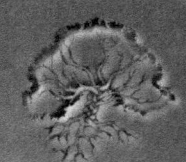

Future Generations

Highlights

My Prayers

ROMANS 15:5

"NOW THE GOD OF PATIENCE AND

CONSOLATION GRANT YOU TO BE LIKEMINDED

ONE TOWARD ANOTHER ACCORDING TO

CHRIST JESUS"

".

Thank You Lord

 Teach Me

Guide Me

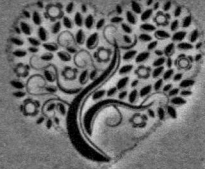

 # Reflect

Is there a Bible verse or a phrase that God has been bringing to your mind a lot lately? What do you think you should do with that information?

_____
_____
_____
_____
_____
_____
_____
_____
_____
_____
_____
_____
_____
_____
_____
_____
_____
_____
_____
_____
_____
_____
_____
_____

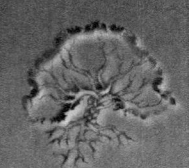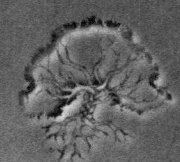

Future Generations

Highlights

My Prayers

DEUTERONOMY 7:9

"KNOW THEREFORE THAT THE LORD THY GOD, HE IS GOD, THE FAITHFUL GOD, WHICH KEEPETH COVENANT AND MERCY WITH THEM THAT LOVE HIM AND KEEP HIS COMMANDMENTS TO A THOUSAND GENERATIONS"

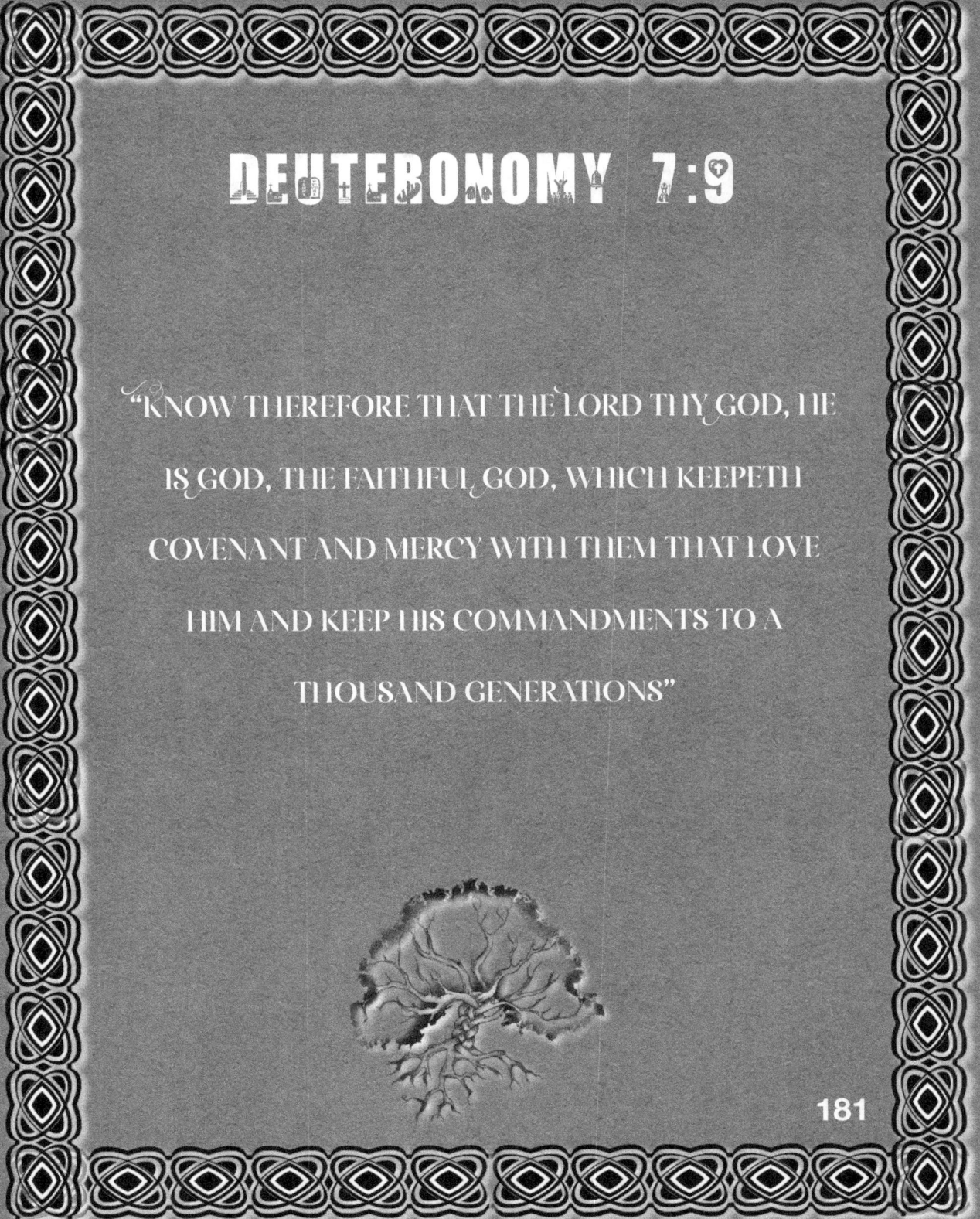

Thank You Lord

Week of: _____

 Teach Me

_____
_____
_____
_____
_____
_____
_____
_____
_____
_____

Guide Me

_____
_____
_____
_____
_____
_____
_____
_____
_____

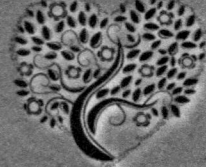

 # Reflect

How does the daily ebb and flow of your emotions affect your

faith? How can you improve in this area?

_____
_____
_____
_____
_____
_____
_____
_____
_____
_____
_____
_____
_____
_____
_____
_____
_____
_____
_____
_____
_____
_____
_____

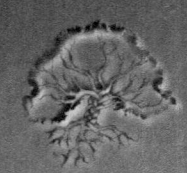

Future Generations

Highlights

My Prayers

HEBREWS 10:23

"LET US HOLD FAST THE PROFESSION OF OUR FAITH WITHOUT WAVERING; (FOR HE IS FAITHFUL THAT PROMISED;)".

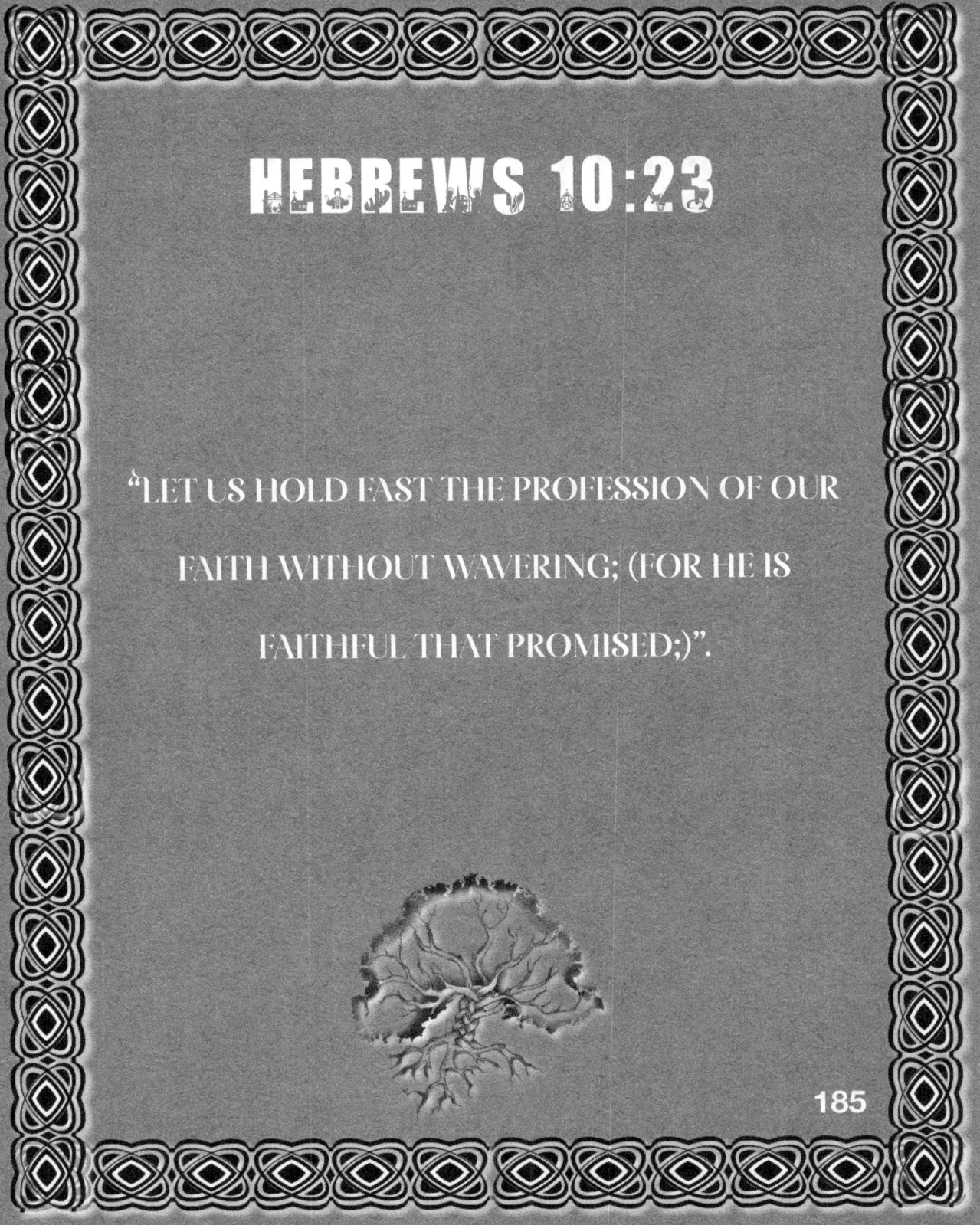

Thank You Lord

Week of: _____

 # Teach Me

_____
_____
_____
_____
_____
_____
_____
_____
_____
_____

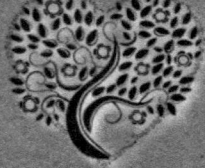

Guide Me

_____
_____
_____
_____
_____
_____
_____
_____
_____
_____
_____

 # Reflect

Do you feel like you are expecting too much from God? Or do you

feel like you are expecting too little from him? Why do you feel

that way?

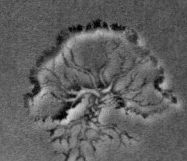

Future Generations

Highlights

My Prayers

PROVERBS 25:28

"HE THAT HATH NO RULE OVER HIS OWN SPIRIT IS

LIKE A CITY THAT IS BROKEN DOWN, AND

WITHOUT WALLS".

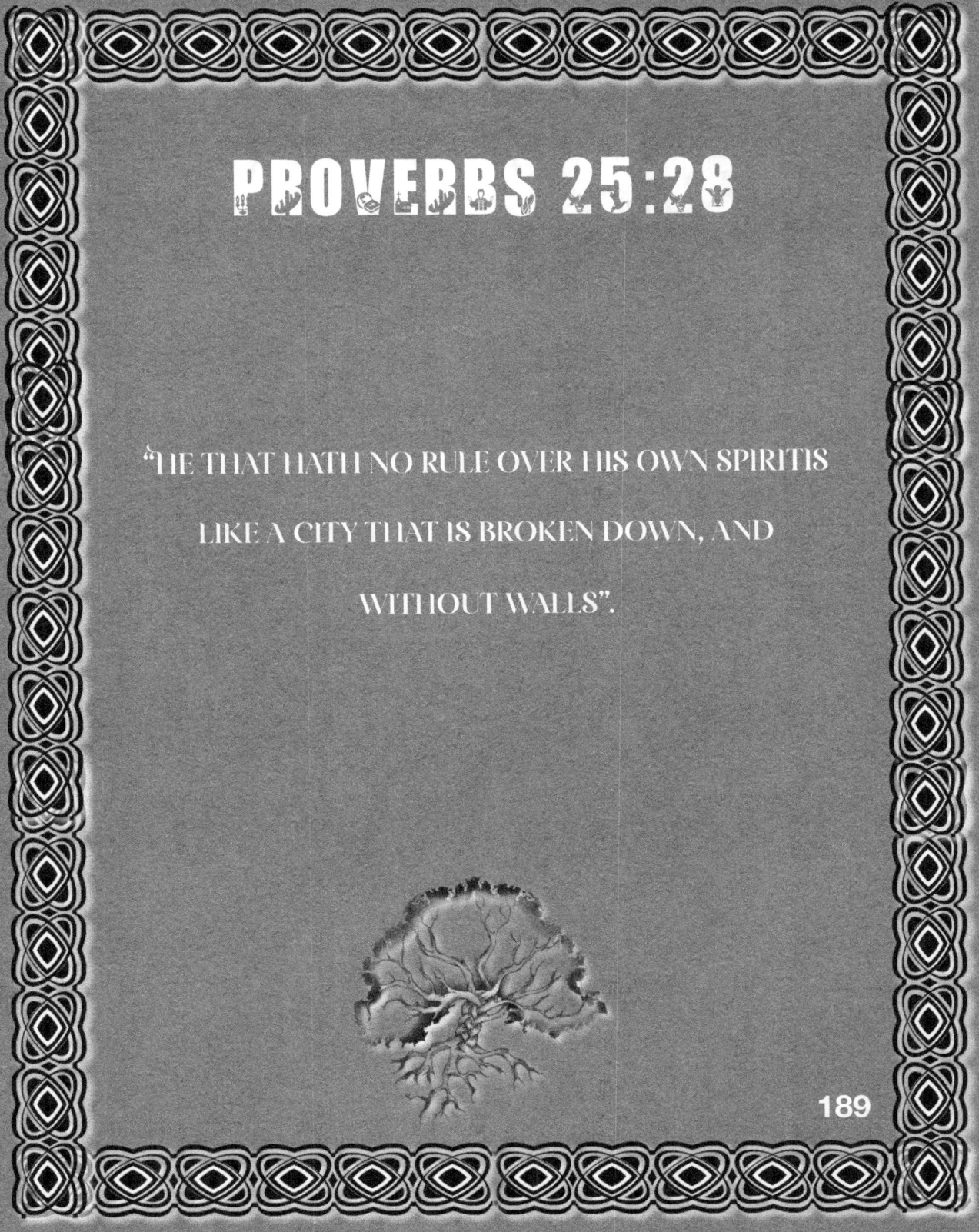

Thank You Lord

Week of: _____

 # Teach Me

_____
_____
_____
_____
_____
_____
_____
_____
_____
_____
_____
_____
_____

 # Guide Me

_____
_____
_____
_____
_____
_____
_____
_____
_____
_____
_____

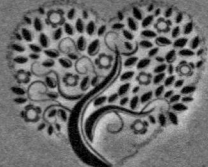

 # Reflect

When you talk to God, do you feel like you are holding back or are

you acting like yourself when you talk to him?

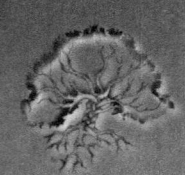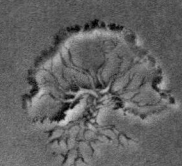

Future Generations

Highlights

My Prayers

2 TIMOTHY 1:7

"FOR GOD HATH NOT GIVEN US THE SPIRIT OF FEAR; BUT OF POWER, AND OF LOVE, AND OF A SOUND MIND".

Thank You Lord

Week of:

 Teach Me

_____
_____
_____
_____
_____
_____
_____
_____
_____
_____

 Guide Me

_____
_____
_____
_____
_____
_____
_____
_____
_____

 # Reflect

What specific prayers, big or small, has God

answered recently?

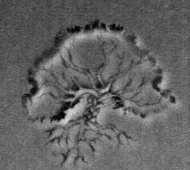

Future Generations

Highlights

My Prayers

JAMES 1:12

"BLESSED IS THE MAN THAT ENDURETH TEMPTATION: FOR WHEN HE IS TRIED, HE SHALL RECEIVE THE CROWN OF LIFE, WHICH THE LORD HATH PROMISED TO THEM THAT LOVE HIM".

Thank You Lord

Week of: _____

 # Teach Me

_____
_____
_____
_____
_____
_____
_____
_____
_____
_____

 # Guide Me

_____
_____
_____
_____
_____
_____
_____
_____
_____
_____
_____

 # Reflect

Write about a time when God sent you a direct

message you couldn't miss.

_____
_____
_____
_____
_____
_____
_____
_____
_____
_____
_____
_____
_____
_____
_____
_____
_____
_____
_____
_____
_____
_____
_____
_____
_____

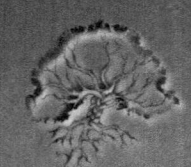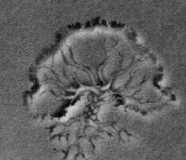

Future Generations

Highlights

My Prayers

MATHEW 26:41

"WATCH AND PRAY, THAT YE ENTER NOT INTO TEMPTATION: THE SPIRIT INDEED IS WILLING, BUT THE FLESH IS WEAK".

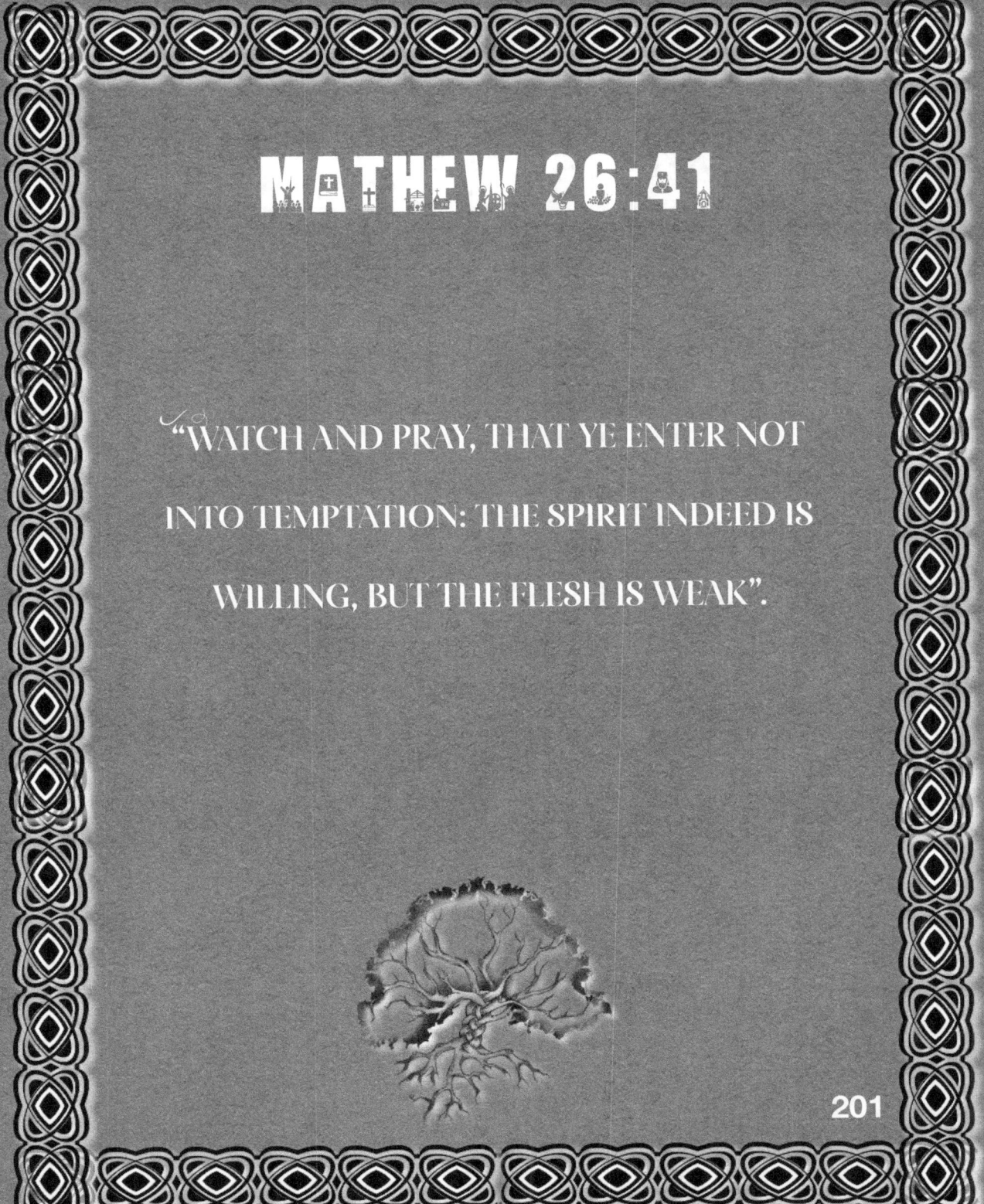

Thank You Lord

 # Teach Me

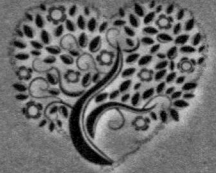 # Guide Me

 # Reflect

The Israelites in Ezekiel's day complained about God being unjust and life being unfair, just as people today do. People ask how God could send someone to hell-especially a person who is trying to do good. Each one of us has sinned, and as a result, we deserve punishment. It is only through God's grace and Jesus' sacrificial death that people can ask for forgiveness and be saved. How do you define justice? How do you define grace?

_____
_____
_____
_____
_____
_____
_____
_____
_____
_____
_____
_____
_____
_____
_____
_____
_____
_____
_____
_____
_____
_____
_____
_____
_____
_____
_____

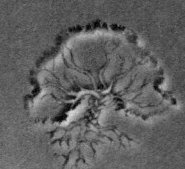

Future Generations

Highlights

My Prayers

PROVERBS 3:5-6

"TRUST IN THE LORD WITH ALL THINE HEART;

AND LEAN NOT UNTO THINE OWN

UNDERSTANDING.

'IN ALL THY WAYS ACKNOWLEDGE HIM,

AND HE SHALL DIRECT THY PATHS"

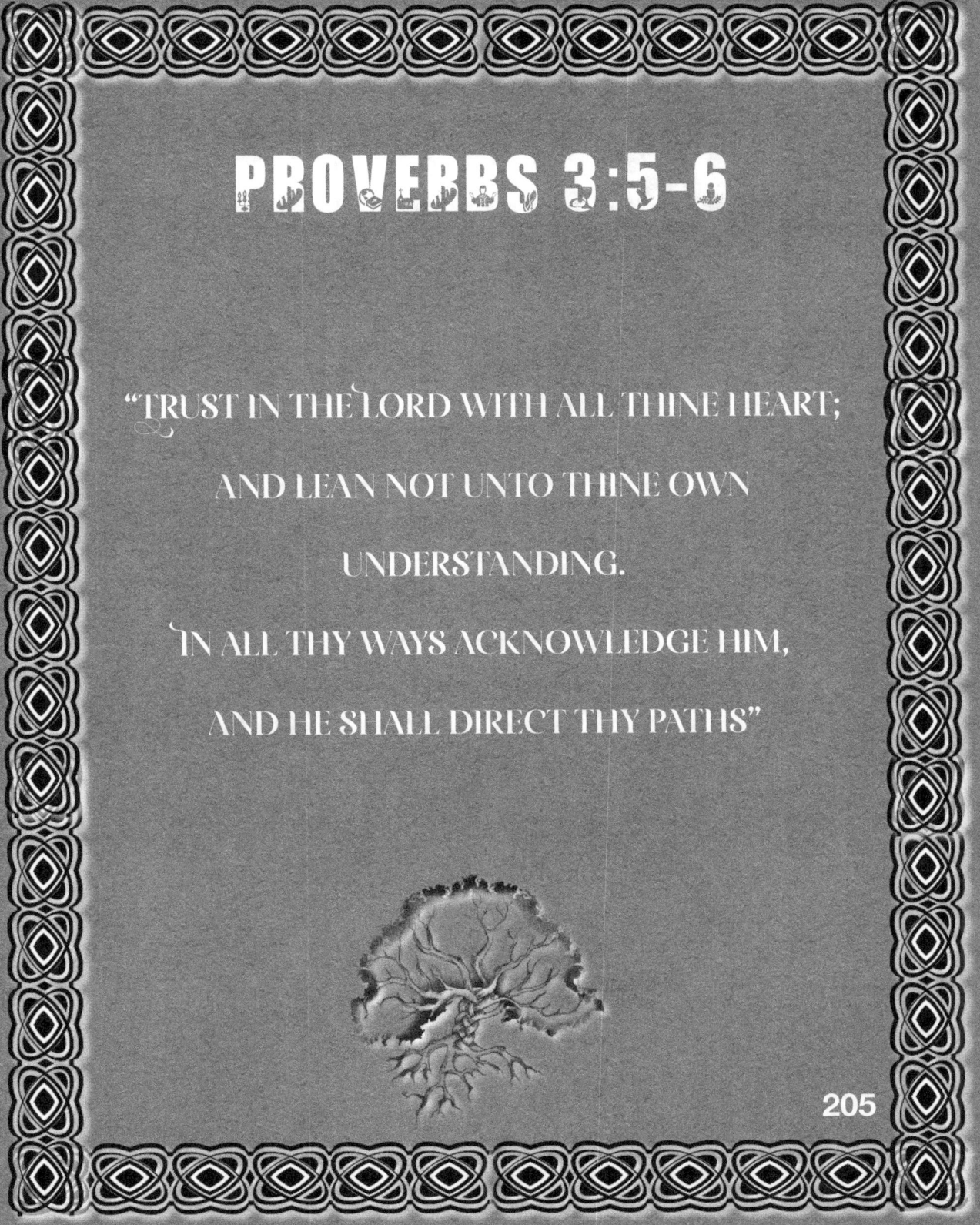

205

Thank You Lord

Week of: _____

 Teach Me

_____
_____
_____
_____
_____
_____
_____
_____
_____
_____
_____
_____
_____

Guide Me

_____
_____
_____
_____
_____
_____
_____
_____
_____
_____
_____
_____

 # Reflect

How are the spaces in which you spend time with God? Is your work, home, and car set up to support your faith?

_____

_____

_____

_____

_____

_____

_____

_____

_____

_____

_____

_____

_____

_____

_____

_____

_____

_____

_____

_____

_____

_____

_____

_____

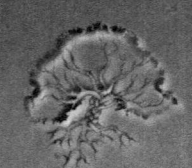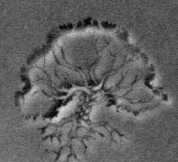

Future Generations

Highlights

My Prayers

PROVERBS 16:3

"COMMIT THY WORKS UNTO THE LORD, AND

THY THOUGHTS SHALL BE ESTABLISHED".

Thank You Lord

Week of:

 # Teach Me

 # Guide Me

 # Reflect

When was the last time you
encouraged someone in their faith?
How did it go? How did it impact
you?

_____

_____

_____

_____

_____

_____

_____

_____

_____

_____

_____

_____

_____

_____

_____

_____

_____

_____

_____

_____

_____

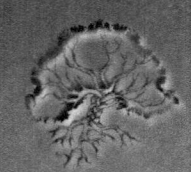 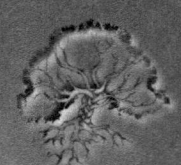

Future Generations

Highlights

My Prayers

JEREMIAH 33:3

"CALL UNTO ME, AND I WILL ANSWER THEE,

AND SHOW THEE GREAT AND MIGHTY

THINGS, WHICH THOU KNOWEST NOT".

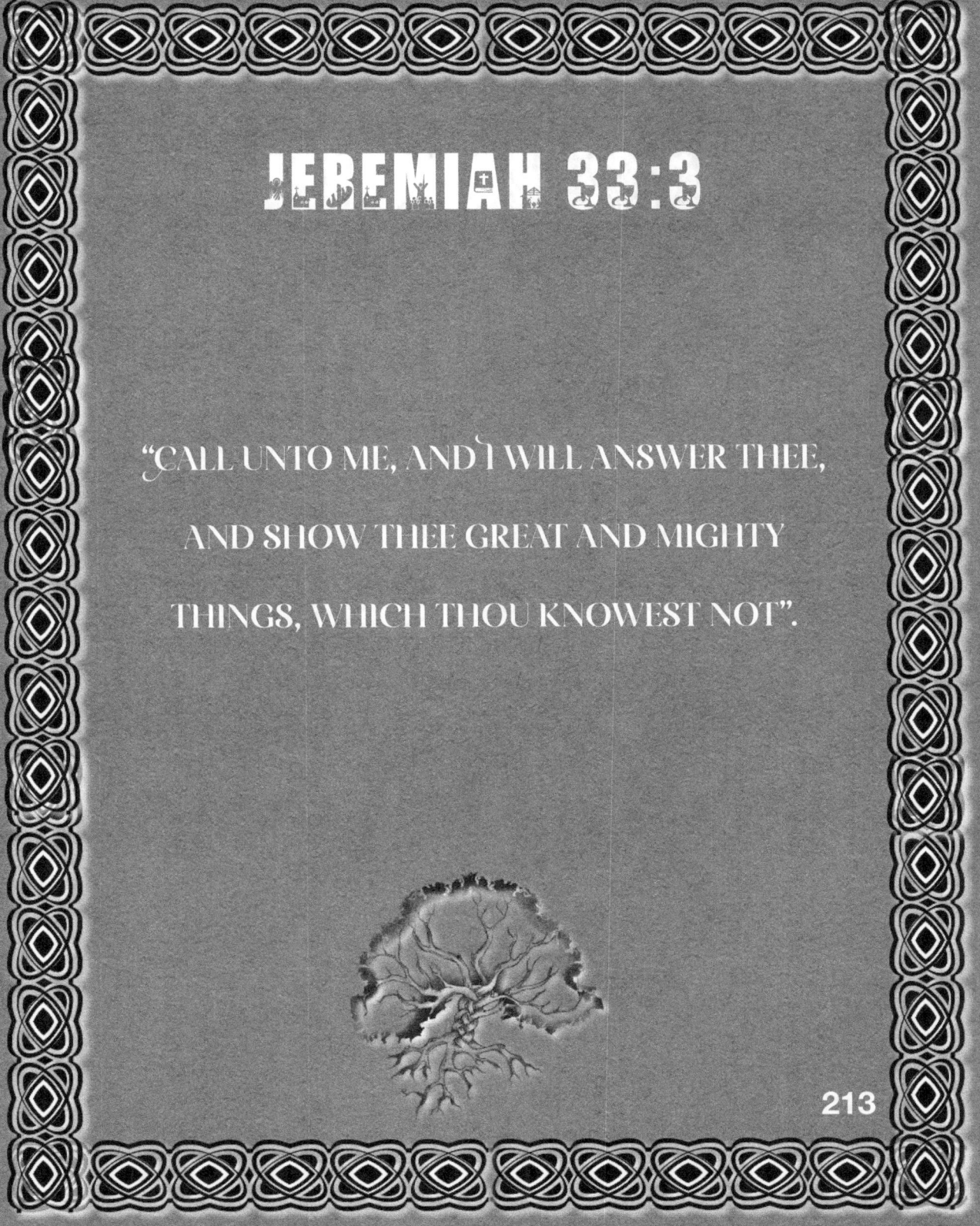

Thank You Lord

Week of: _____

 # Teach Me

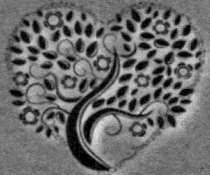

Guide Me

 # Reflect

> **Romans 8:28**
> " We know that all things work together for good to those who love
> God, to those who are the called according to His purpose"
>
> **Life hardly ever takes a straight path. What does this passage say
> about all the detours your life might take?**

_____

_____

_____

_____

_____

_____

_____

_____

_____

_____

_____

_____

_____

_____

_____

_____

_____

_____

_____

_____

_____

_____

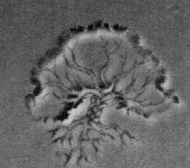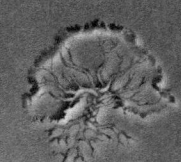

Future Generations

Highlights

My Prayers

PROVERBS 4:7

"WISDOM IS THE PRINCIPAL THING; THEREFORE

GET WISDOM:

AND WITH ALL THY GETTING GET

UNDERSTANDING".

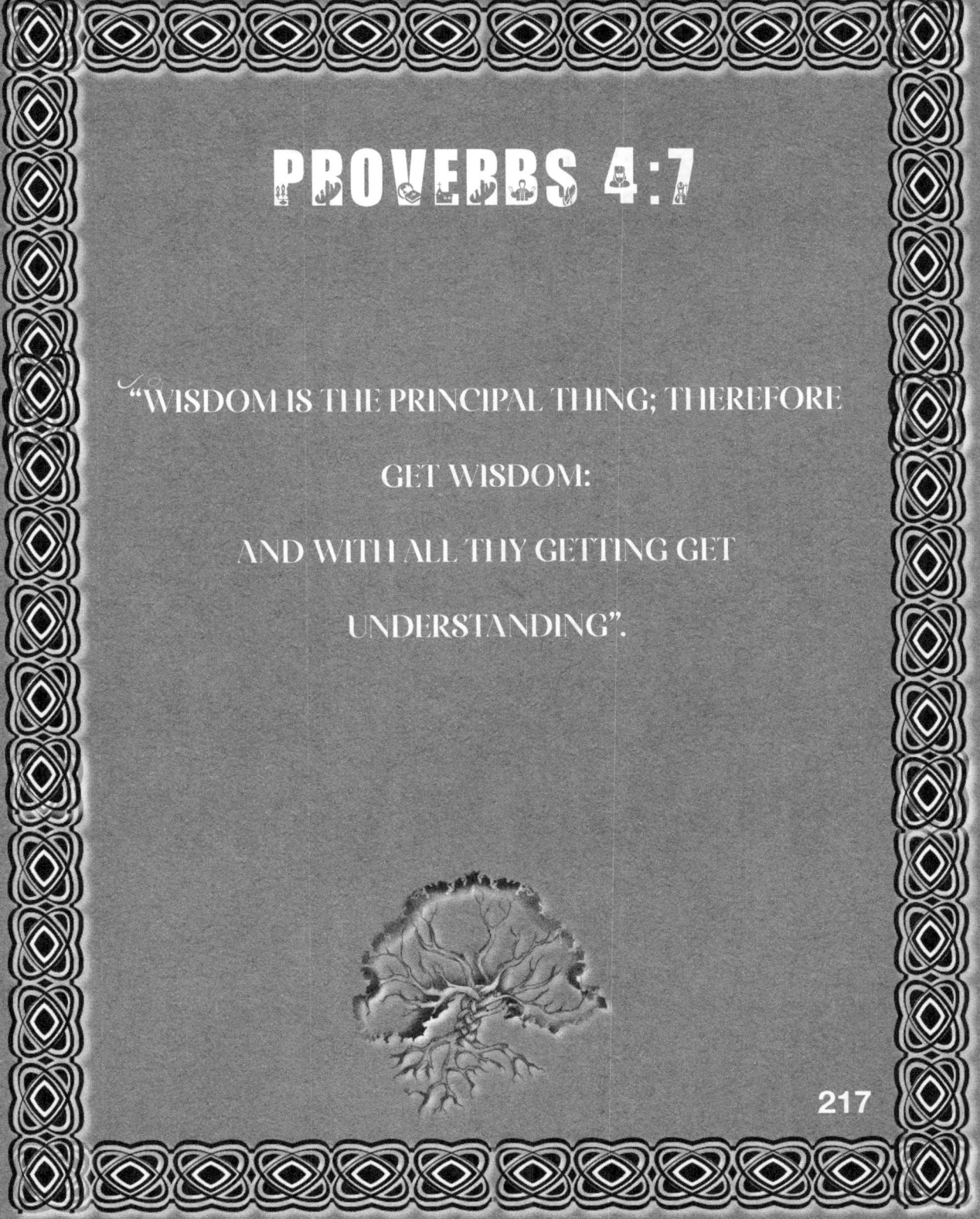

Thank You Lord

Week of: _____

 ## Teach Me

_____
_____
_____
_____
_____
_____
_____
_____
_____

 ## Guide Me

_____
_____
_____
_____
_____
_____
_____
_____
_____

 # Reflect

Stepping out in faith isn't always easy. What would you tell someone who is about to step out on faith?

Future Generations

Highlights

My Prayers

2 CORINTHIANS 12:10

" THEREFORE I TAKE PLEASURE IN

INFIRMITIES, IN REPROACHES, IN

NECESSITIES, IN PERSECUTIONS, IN

DISTRESSES FOR CHRIST'S SAKE: FOR

WHEN I AM WEAK, THEN AM I STRONG.".

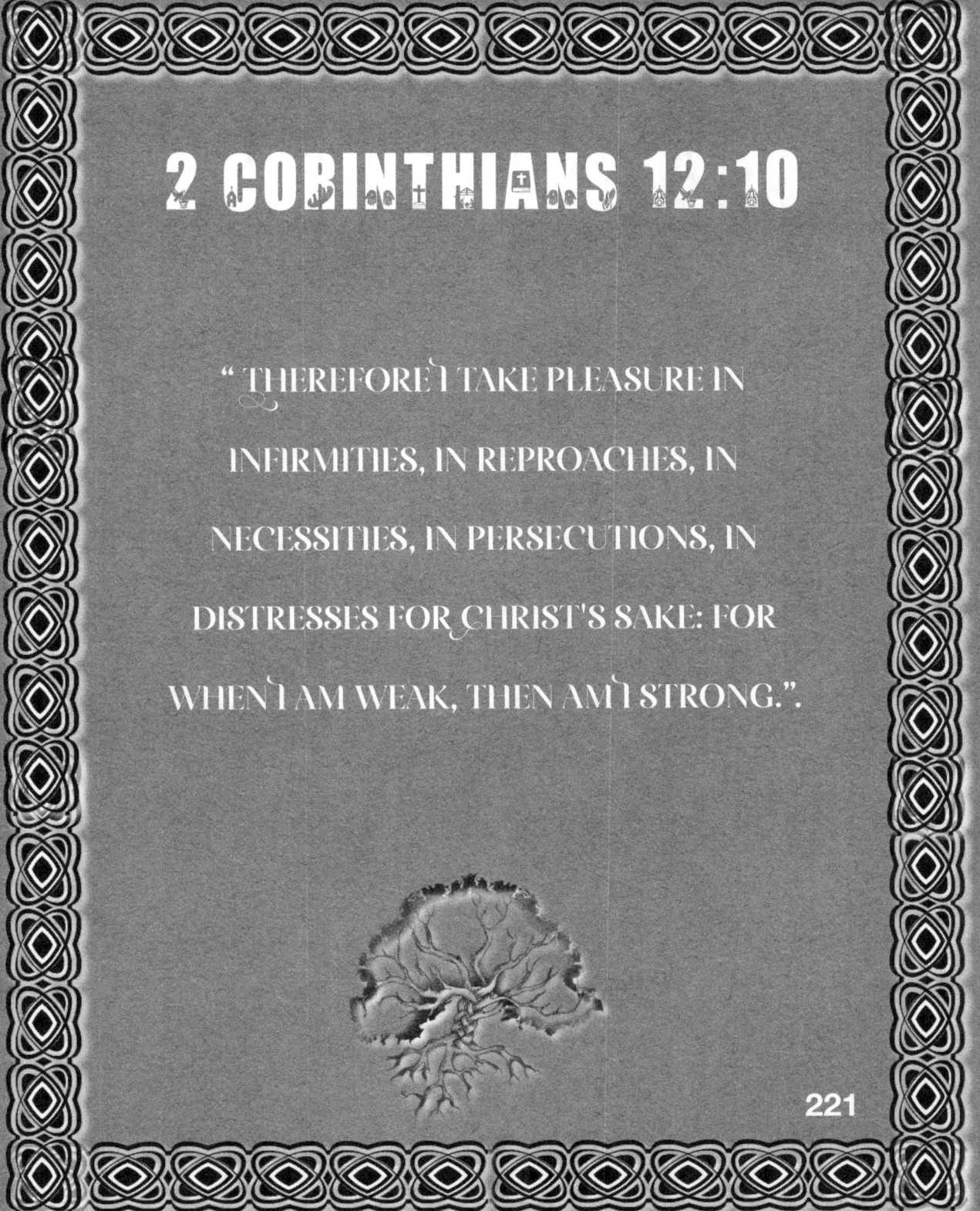

Thank You Lord

 # Teach Me

 # Guide Me

 # Reflect

> Do you feel like you are used all of the talents God gave you this year? If not, what could you change so that you are using them?

_____
_____
_____
_____
_____
_____
_____
_____
_____
_____
_____
_____
_____
_____
_____
_____
_____
_____
_____
_____
_____
_____
_____

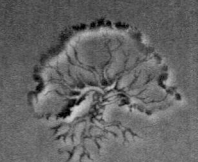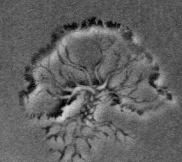

Future Generations

Highlights

My Prayers

Prayers

Prayers

 # Prayers

Prayers